To Love a Child

TO LOVE A CHILD

A Complete Guide to Adoption, Foster Parenting, and Other Ways to Share Your Life with Children

Marianne Takas & Edward Warner

Addison-Wesley Publishing Company

Reading, Massachusetts • Menlo Park, California • New York
Don Mills, Ontario • Wokingham, England • Amsterdam • Bonn
Sydney • Singapore • Tokyo • Madrid • San Juan
Paris • Seoul • Milan • Mexico City • Taipei

Library of Congress Cataloging-in-Publication Data

Takas, Marianne.
To love a child : a complete guide to adoption, foster parenting, and other ways to share your life with children / Marianne Takas, Edward Warner.
p. cm.
Includes index.
ISBN 0-201-55083-0
1. Adoption—United States. 2. Foster parents—United States.
I. Warner, Edward, 1953– II. Title.
HV875.55.T35 1992
362.7'33'0973—dc20 92-12609
CIP

Text design by Richard Oriolo

Set in 11-point Goudy Old Style by Pagesetters

1 2 3 4 5 6 7 8 9-MW-95949392
First printing, August 1992

To the adults who were there for us when we were children, and the children who enrich our lives now.

Contents

Introduction

This book began as a professional project, a collaboration between an attorney specializing in child welfare issues and a professional journalist. It quickly became a labor of love.

We were inspired, first, by the people we interviewed. We talked to professionals and activists within the field, many of whom are also biological, adoptive, and/or foster parents. We talked to caring adults from all walks of life who had built meaningful lives with children in a variety of ways. We also talked to children, and to young adults who had grown up with adoptive and/or foster families. All had insights to share, and shared them generously.

We came to know many deeply happy people who had found joy and strength in a variety of adoptive, fostering, and mentoring relationships. Few had grown up envisioning the path they had taken, and many had experienced disappointments in getting there. Yet most embraced the lives they had built. The families we met—like most families, but perhaps more so—were filled with love and anger and joy and frustration and hope.

Most were proud of their lives and their families, and did not ask us to change their names or identifying details in the text. We decided to do so anyway, for the privacy of the children involved. Books stay in print for years, and children have differing privacy needs as they grow older. A few accounts, either for privacy reasons or to communicate a typical issue, involve composites of more than one family's experience. Professionals cited as experts, of course, are always identified by their actual names and affiliations.

As we explored the issues of parenting, we found ourselves touched in deep and personal ways. For Ed, who spent a short part of his childhood with a caring foster family, and thereafter was raised primarily by his aunt and uncle, it meant reexperiencing those important relationships. There were some poignant and even painful moments, unraveling reasons and events that had never been fully explained before. There were also some very happy discoveries. Ed had always, for example, remembered his first foster family with special fondness and amazing clarity. The day he'd arrived, five years old and frightened, they'd taken him and the other children in their home to McDonald's (back when McDonald's was new and terribly exciting) to celebrate his arrival. It had given him a message of welcome, of being worth a celebration. He'd always wanted to thank them, and to let them know he'd grown up to be happy and healthy. When he confided in a foster parent, interviewed for this book, the hesitation ended. At the woman's urging, he searched for and (surprisingly easily) found this family, and reopened an old friendship.

For Marianne as well, exploring the range of parenting relationships meant revisiting important childhood relationships. At first the connection was less obvious, because she'd been raised by her own biological parents. Yet always, and especially once Marianne and her siblings were grown, her mother had found ways to be a part of other children's lives. To this day, those relationships remain strong and meaningful. Writing this book clarified for Marianne how much her mother's unspoken but powerful message—that all children are our children—had helped to define her own life and work.

The most important effect we experienced was the impact on our own thinking, as a happily married couple, about parenting. To the best of our knowledge, biological parenting is an option open to us. Because we both love children, and love the idea of creating a child together, the option is an attractive one. We have realized more and more, though, that it's not our only option, nor the only attractive one. Fostering, adoption, and biological parenting are quite different from one another, and each has its own challenges, meaning, and joys. We would love someday to have—like some of the families we came to know—a family that includes children both by birth and by adoption. Most immediately, however, we have decided to become foster parents. It is, for us, one of the most exciting decisions we have ever made.

On the road to making our decision, we had a chance to struggle with a few barriers. Most potent was the idea, all around us in subtle ways, that "real" parenting is the most important parenting, and "our" children are the most important children.

We began, for example, to volunteer in programs with children, including a local youth recreation program and a local kindergarten. Frequently, these commitments required us to take time from our work in the middle of the workweek. Since we were both self-employed at the time, this was fairly easy to arrange—but we found ourselves doing so more or less secretively, telling colleagues, for example, "I can't meet Monday morning. I have, uh, an appointment." Other attorneys or journalists might arrange a four-day workweek to have time for their "own" children, but it seemed somehow less acceptable to do so for "other people's" children.

Finally, we realized that we were avoiding an issue central to our beliefs. If we truly believe—as we do—that all children are equally deserving of time, caring, and commitment, it is essential to act on that belief, and to do so without apology. We began mentioning our involvements openly, saying, for example, "No, I can't be in court that day. I'm at a kindergarten Monday mornings." And "No, I don't represent them. I do sometimes color with them, or show them how to use the bubble maker."

Later, when we began to think about foster parenting, we discussed it with our friends and families. Not everyone understood; some people assumed we were infertile, and some who knew we weren't asked why we "didn't want to have children." Yet most were willing to listen, and responded thoughtfully when we explained that we *did* want to have children in our lives, and we felt foster parenting was one of several exciting and satisfying ways to do so. As we began explaining why the choice was so meaningful to us, most were supportive.

If writing this book was a journey, we did not travel alone. At every step of the way, we received generous help, support, and guidance. Although there are many to whom we owe thanks, a few deserve special mention. Gordon Evans of the National Foster Parent Association, Patricia Ryan of the Institute for the Study of Children and Families at Eastern Michigan University, Mark Hardin of the American Bar Association Center on Children and the Law, Gloria Hochman of the National Adoption Center, Dawn Smith-Pliner of Friends in Adoption, and Clarice Walker of the District of Columbia Department of Human Services each contributed in a major, substantial way to the book—not only sharing their expertise, ideas, and resources, but reading and commenting on drafts. Without their help, this would be a far less useful book.

If there is one person who most deserves our thanks, it is Eileen Mayers Pasztor of the Child Welfare League of America. Eileen is a leading expert in the field, who didn't know us when we called to ask for help, and she could have accurately said she was too busy. Instead she spent hours sharing her ideas, giving us resources, involving us in committees, and reading drafts. Indeed, she made so many helpful suggestions that we sometimes despaired of ever making all the improvements she suggested. Along the way, she became a dear and valued friend. We cannot thank her enough.

Finally, our thanks go to each of the families who opened their hearts to tell us their stories. We hope that they will inspire and touch your lives as they touched ours.

To Love a Child

One

The Joys of Family

There's one way to make a baby, but many ways to make a family.

—social worker comment
original source unknown

With America's second baby boom in full swing, more and more people are experiencing the joys of nurturing a child. Many of the joys are timeless, as true now as always: the warmth of loving, the wonder of watching a child grow, the satisfaction of making a contribution. Yet much has changed, too. Although biological parenting remains the most common route, hundreds of thousands of caring adults today choose other ways to build a life with children. Adoption, foster parenting, and various forms of child mentoring enrich the lives of countless children and adults.

It is true that many, if not most, people begin with an assumption and a hope that they will someday have a child biologically. If this becomes an unrealistic option, due to infertility, age, health risks, or other factors, feelings of sadness, anger, and a sense of loss are common, especially initially.

If this is your situation, you should know that you are not alone. An estimated ten to fifteen million married couples in America today are either involuntarily childless, or involuntarily limited to fewer children than they wish. Additional millions of child-loving adults may feel foreclosed from traditional childraising because they are single, divorced, gay, or beyond their childbearing years. Still others have one or more children but feel the desire to extend their families to include other children.

Even more important, you should know that the most basic core of your dream—to care for and nurture a child or children—is absolutely, unquestionably both possible and practical, without waiting, without scheming, and without spending money you can't afford. This is true whether you are married or single, elderly or a young adult, gay or straight, and wealthy or of limited income.

In part this is because the number of children needing an adult to care for them still far exceeds the availability of adults ready, willing, and able to provide that care. So, although your own life circumstances may influence the type and nature of the relationship you choose, the opportunity for a life filled with the joy and meaning of parenting is available to every caring, responsible adult who wishes it.

To say that there is, right now, a child waiting for you would be an understatement. More accurately, there are one or three or even several children waiting—as many as you have room for in your life and in your heart.

If this is the case, why is there a common perception of childless couples and singles doomed to empty nests, exorbitant adoption fees, and long waiting lists? The simple answer is that families have changed dramatically in recent decades, with resulting changes in the needs of children and the role of potential adoptive parents. A generation ago, the average child needing alternate parenting was a white infant available for immediate adoption, without identified health problems and without an established or ongoing relationship with the biological family. Today a child in need of parenting may be any race or any age, may have physical or emotional difficulties, and may have and wish to maintain at least some form of relationship with parents, siblings, or other family members. Older child adoption, foster parenting, and child and family mentoring are now far more commonly needed than adoption of an infant.

Yet, while the needs of the children have changed dramatically, the focus of most adults hoping to parent has been much slower to change. The reasons for the unshifting focus on infant adoption are understandable (for example, a desire to be similar to families formed by birth, a lack of familiarity with the alternatives, and possible lack of confidence in nontraditional situations), but the result is often sadly missed connections.

Each year about two million couples attempt to adopt; about 3 percent succeed. Many of the rest spend years in heartbreaking frustration. Yet, even as large numbers of adults compete desperately and often painfully to adopt a small number of available European American babies without identified health problems, equally large numbers of desperately lonely children are growing up in need of caring and nurturance. The lost potential is incalculable, as adults and children who could have built families together remain instead frustrated and apart.

If you are—or are able to become—flexible in your image of what you have to offer a child, your opportunities to build a life rich with children are immediate and vast. This book is about all the options: infant adoption, but also older child adoption, foster parenting, and child and family mentoring. It is about infants and toddlers, grade schoolers and teens; about children with and without serious physical, emotional, or behavioral challenges. Most of all, it is simply about children—real kids, with real needs—and how you can meaningfully intertwine your life with theirs.

Extending your family to include a child or children is one of the most important and life-changing decisions you may ever make. It is also, in today's world, an increasingly complex one. Many people who begin with a specific goal in mind find, as they begin to pursue it, that their perspectives change—perhaps because of unexpected setbacks in their initial route, or because they learn more about other alternatives, or some combination of both. Priorities and values may become clearer, and choices that appeared settled at the outset may be reconsidered.

The Needs of Children Today

The first step in exploring your options for alternate parenting is to understand more about the needs of children today. As we examine this issue, we'll look at some rough estimates of how many children are in need of the various types of alternate parenting so that you can get a better sense of where the greatest need and opportunity lie. The estimates, gathered from the national resources listed in the appendix, are inexact because, for the most part, our country does not keep as careful statistics on children's needs, as it does in so many other areas.

A full understanding of children's needs must begin with the circumstances of their families of birth. Millions of children in our country today, and many more millions worldwide, are born to families that are under stress due to poverty, parental separation, homelessness, substance abuse, extreme youth of the parents, or other social and family problems. Many of these children are raised to adulthood by their parents, who may show surprising strengths in meeting the challenges facing them. Many others are partially or largely raised by their parents of birth but need extra supports their parents can't offer, such as temporary foster care in times of family crisis, or a long-term mentoring relationship with a stable and caring adult. Some cannot be raised to adulthood by their parents, and need adoption.

Sometimes parents will decide early on, during the child's infancy or even before the child's birth, to place the child for adoption. Although there are many exceptions, European American infants are often placed through private adoption agencies or through what are known as identified adoptions, and African American and Native American infants are often placed through the public adoption agencies of state social services departments. Additionally, some infants or young children from other nations are adopted by U.S. citizens, usually through private agencies specializing in international adoption.

Each year about 10,000 to 15,000 U.S.-born and about 10,000 foreign-born infants and very young children are adopted in the United States.

Sometimes children are placed for adoption not during infancy but at later ages. This can occur through voluntary placement by a parent, usually the mother, who develops severe problems and feels that the child needs a permanent home with more stable parenting. Placement for adoption can also follow the death or permanent disability of the responsible parent. Additionally, many children are placed for adoption after their parents' parental rights have been legally terminated by the state social services department because of parental abuse, neglect, or inability to care for the child.

Each year about 35,000 to 40,000 children older than infants are adopted, generally through either public or private adoption agencies. At any given time, thousands of older children, particularly those with special needs or in sibling groups, are immediately available for adoption.

Most children are not placed for adoption, of course, but are raised by their families of birth. And most families offer their children the best they can: a mix of love and strength, shortcomings and limitations. When family stress becomes too high, they often need help.

Foster parenting is a major form of alternate parenting that provides caring, stable, family-type care to children whose families are under severe stress. Children may be placed into foster care voluntarily by their parent(s), or involuntarily because of parental abuse or neglect. Foster care is intended to be temporary, lasting until the parent(s) can, with help, address the family's problems, allowing the child to return home safely. That may take a few weeks, a few months, or a few years. During the time that a child is with a foster parent, the foster parent fulfills all the roles of parenting: caring, guiding, teaching, disciplining. Sometimes the child's family of origin is not able to solve its problems, and the child is adopted—often by the family that has been providing foster care. In fact, most families that foster parent over a period of years at some point have an opportunity to adopt a child or children in foster care with them.

At any given time, about 360,000 children of all ages are in foster care, and caring foster parents are always needed.

The greatest number of children do not need adoption or even foster parenting, but do need an additional caring adult in their lives on a stable, long-term basis. One of the most meaningful methods for fulfilling this role is known as child and family mentoring. Child and family mentoring is much like becoming a part of the child's extended family, such as an aunt, uncle, or grandparent. The mentor builds a relationship with the child directly, but in a way that respects and affirms the child's existing family ties. Less established than adoption and foster parenting, mentoring is now emerging in many social service programs as a formal and important role in meeting the needs of children and their families.

Literally millions of children need, and are not yet receiving, child and family mentoring.

Avoiding Misinformation

Although adoption and foster care are common, a surprising number of myths and misunderstandings have arisen about them. We'll look at some of the myths and replace them with accurate information.

Myth: People adopt only if they can't have a biological child. They foster parent only if they can't adopt.

Fact: People adopt and foster parent because they love children and want to expand their family life. Each form of parenting has its own joys and challenges, and may appeal to different people for different reasons.

Infertility is a factor in many, but not all, decisions to adopt. Some people have one or more children biologically, then chose to adopt. Some people would rather adopt a child without a permanent family than create a new child. For some people who were themselves adopted, adoption may seem the most meaningful choice.

Foster parents have many motivations, but, according to the National Foster Parent Association, few report that they made their choice as a result of unsuccessful attempts at childbirth and adoption. In fact, a very large proportion of foster parents also have biological and/or adoptive children. For some, foster parenting is an opportunity to have an impact: to reach more children than traditional parenting alone could offer, and to do so at a crucial time in the child's life. For others, who may have been in foster care themselves as children or were otherwise helped by some special adult who changed their lives, it may offer a chance to pass on some of what they received. For some people who just love kids, it is a way to keep the house full of children for years on end, without overpopulating the world or taking on more financial responsibility than they are able to handle. It may also be, for anyone who has love to give but is not able to commit for the next ten or twenty years (whether due to age, marital status, or other reasons), a wonderful chance to care for a child who needs it today.

All that said, it is probably true that many people who

once hoped to give birth end up adopting instead, and that some who once hoped to adopt decide to foster parent. This may involve the painful letting go of a dream, first of childbirth and perhaps then of adoption. That progression of choices, however, says nothing about how meaningful any one route will ultimately turn out to be. Practical realities may have a hand in determining which form of parenting we ultimately choose, but all three—birthparenting, adoption, and foster parenting—have been deeply satisfying to many, many families.

Myth: The problem with adoption, especially of older children, is that you don't get that parent-infant bonding, so the relationship is always incomplete. As for foster parenting, it is just too painful to keep loving children you'll only lose.

Fact: Both of these concerns are understandable, and sometimes they do create difficulties. Yet adoptive and foster parents themselves tend to see both very much in perspective.

The answer to the parent-infant bonding concern seems to be that love has a wonderful way of making do with what is available. There are plenty of other ways to bond, and they happen every day. Adoptive family relationships may have their challenges, but most people—adoptive parents and children—seem to experience them as family attachments as meaningful as any other.

In the very interesting and readable *Making Decisions About Children* (T. J. Press, 1990, pp. 37–47), Professor H. Rudolph Schaffer reviews studies from his native England and Europe exploring the ability of later-adopted children to form loving attachments with their adoptive parents. Although the children in the studies, many of whom had been raised in orphanages for their early years and had had as many as fifty caregivers, tended to exhibit difficulties (such as behavior problems, academic problems, and problems relating to peers), almost all appeared, with time, to form loving attachments with their adoptive parents. "It seems," concluded the author, "that children up to the age of 7 at least can successfully be integrated into a family, despite a complete lack of previous personal relationships." The mention of age seven, incidentally, did not imply negative results with older children; rather, no data were available on children adopted at older ages.

Although the concern about the pain of loving and losing children in foster care seems to make sense, it is most often voiced by people who have never been foster parents. Foster parents themselves report that, although it isn't always easy, it definitely is possible to care deeply about children in foster care, enjoy them immensely, and let them go.

"That's a part of foster parenting," explained one experienced foster mother, "and you have to understand that from the beginning. I'm also a teacher, and you'd be surprised how you get to care about your students. So I cry at the end of every school year, and I cry every time one of the children in foster care with me leaves. But that's a part of living. I'm not going to stop loving these kids, or giving them whatever I can—and I've never died yet from crying."

The process of dating, love, and marriage provides another analogy that might be helpful. Although almost everyone's first reaction in thinking about foster parenting is "Oh, I could never bear the pain of letting go," very few people have that reaction about the idea of dating and falling in love. Yet most people do fall in love with, or at least grow to care very deeply for, people whom they do not then marry—

and they do not necessarily regret the experience. It almost seems that we are willing to think about other adults as separate individuals, but are socially trained to think about caring for children only in the context of guaranteeing that they are "ours" forever.

This is not to suggest, of course, that saying goodbye to a child who is leaving foster care is easy. Among both foster parents and mental health professionals involved with foster families, separation grief is commonly mentioned as an important and challenging issue. It is probably accurate to say that, *for some people*, foster parenting is not a good choice, because for them it would likely lead to excessively painful grieving or defensive withholding of affection.

Many foster parents have developed good support systems for dealing with the challenge, however, and find that the joys of loving more than outweigh the pain of moving on when their work as a foster parent is done. Some also report that they'd rather be there for a child who needs them than be frightened off by the fact that they can't "keep" the child.

Myth: Children adopted at older ages, or children in foster care, are deeply maladjusted and extremely difficult to care for. On the other hand, if you adopt a healthy baby, you can be assured of having a child without serious problems.

Fact: A wide variety of children are in foster care or are available for adoption at all ages. Although some have serious behavior problems, others do not. According to Patricia Ryan, administrative director of the Institute for the Study of Children and Families at Eastern Michigan University (and an adoptive mother), almost all children in foster care or being adopted can respond to consistent and caring discipline and limit-setting.

Some people have the impression that foster care is a

"dumping ground" for children who are out of control. This, explains Ryan, is a complete misunderstanding. Rather, foster care allows children to enjoy a safe family atmosphere while their own parents work on resolving pressing life problems. Children who are so out of control as to be a danger to themselves or others should not be cared for in foster families; they need a more structured environment than most families can provide.

At the same time, it is fair to say that some children in foster care or available for adoption do have serious emotional and behavioral problems. Eileen Mayers Pasztor, family foster care director for the Child Welfare League of America (and a foster and adoptive mother), notes that a major cause of difficulty for some new adoptive and foster parents is lack of preparation and unrealistic expectations. "People like to say 'Love is all you need,' " explains Pasztor, "but that's just not true. Some of these children have serious problems, and help and training and support is what you need as well."

It is important to find out as much as possible about a child before accepting the role of that child's foster parent, and doubly important if you are considering adoption. If you believe that a child's needs are beyond what you can handle, it is right and appropriate *not* to take the child into your care.

At the same time, regarding adoption in particular, it is important to realize that the commitment is an extremely serious one and that no form of adoption is without risk. In fact, adoption of an infant, often believed to be a guarantee of a "clean slate," may actually entail some risks greater than those in the adoption of an older child. Some disabilities may not show up in an infant, but may prove to be quite severe as the child reaches later developmental stages. For example, a history of prenatal drug or alcohol exposure may not be known, and may not be apparent in an infant, but the effects can be disabling as the child grows older.

So, although foster parents should not commit to care for a child whose known needs are beyond their capacity, the responsibility in adoption is even greater. You should accept the responsibility of adopting a child only if you are truly willing to stand by that commitment in sickness and in health.

Be aware, however, that as you explore the question of what types of children you have the capacity to parent well, you can obtain help. Most agencies placing children into either foster care or adoption have preparation and training programs that meet this need. One excellent program, used by agencies in many states with people considering either fostering or adoption, is the Model Approach to Partnerships in Parenting (MAPP), developed by the Child Welfare Institute of Atlanta, Georgia. Another fine program, used for those considering fostering, is the Foster Parent Education Series, developed by the Institute for the Study of Children and Families.

A good training program will aid in self-evaluation and support shared decision making. It should help you to learn about the needs of children in foster care or available for adoption, what services are available to you locally in meeting those needs, and what would be required of you. Clear, complete information can be a real comfort and a practical help.

Ultimately, the only valid generalization that can be made about children available for adoption or foster care is that they are, quite simply, children. They may have unexpected problems and may bring unexpected joys. Like other children, they need, benefit from, and may flourish under love and caring.

Myth: Adoption is the more conventional choice. Foster parenting is an unusual choice compared with adoption.

Fact: You have already seen the numbers, so you know this belief isn't true. Each year, about 60,000 children, including older children and those from other countries, are adopted in the United States. Yet about 360,000 children are currently in foster care, and thousands enter each week, as others leave. Adoption may be discussed more often, but foster parenting is actually far more common.

If you have been relatively unaware of foster parenting but have heard a lot about adoption, there are a number of likely reasons. One is related to how media coverage is affected by socioeconomic issues. Traditionally, formal adoption has been more common among upper- and upper-middle-income families, foster parenting has been more common among middle- and lower-middle-income families, and informal (nonlegal) adoption has occurred most frequently among lower-income families. Since journalists, editors, talk show hosts, and television producers all tend to be from an upper- or upper-middle-income background, they are more likely to be personally involved, or acquainted with others involved, with formal adoption. Not surprisingly, they are therefore more likely to think of featuring it than foster parenting or informal arrangements. If you also happen to be from a middle-upper- or upper-income background, you, too, may know more people who have been involved in adoption than in foster parenting.

Unfortunately, the lack of equal awareness about all options can make it harder to choose what is right for you. You may get full information about your options in this book and through other resources you seek out, but you'll probably discuss your decision with family and friends. They may not be equally well informed about all types of alternate parenting—and, more seriously, may have prejudices based on misinformation. Even among many support groups and informational meetings for infertile adults, participants may not be equally well informed about all options.

Fortunately, there are advocacy groups devoted to every type of option discussed in this book. They are listed in the appendix, and can help you to learn more, and to get a more balanced perspective.

Interestingly, the socioeconomic differences between typical adoptive and foster parents may be changing. According to the Child Welfare League of America, there is evidence that younger foster parents being approved and certified in recent years have higher levels of education than their predecessors. As more states implement foster parent training, and as more foster parents organize and demand professional treatment, foster parenting will likely become increasingly attractive to people of all income levels. At the same time, health care subsidies and waiver of adoption fees for children with special needs are making formal adoption more widely available among middle- and lower-income families.

Cultural Issues in Adoption and Foster Care

Another important issue in adoption and foster care is the cultural needs of children. This is crucial both because cultural heritage is so important in itself and because our society as a whole often fails to value all races and cultures equally.

The issue arises in part because, in our country, African

Americans, Native Americans, and Hispanic Americans are disproportionately affected by racism, poverty, and all the ills that go with them, such as homelessness, joblessness, family stress, and substance abuse. Then, when they do experience family problems, they are less likely to receive the services they need to address the problems. Not surprisingly, they therefore experience higher rates of family breakdown and parent/child disruption. This means that a disproportionate number of children needing adoption or foster parenting are from these minority groups. In fact, according to the American Public Welfare Association, children of these groups are disproportionately represented in the foster care system by a margin of more than two to one.

This societal problem, although important in itself, also leads to pressing questions about how best to meet the needs of the many minority children who need foster parenting or adoption. Most people agree that a child's cultural identity is important, and that adoptive or foster parents of the same culture are generally best suited to helping the child learn about and take pride in that culture. In a society where racism is still a daily reality, minority parents are also generally best equipped to help the child learn to address racism without loss of pride or confidence. Finally, minority adopters and foster parents, particularly if they are relatives or from the child's own community, may be better able to help heal the child's sense of loss and alienation after a parent/child disruption.

For all these reasons, caseworkers seeking to place an African American, Hispanic, Native American, or mixed race child will almost always try first to find an adoptive or foster parent of similar heritage. If you are a member of one of these groups, you will likely find children of your culture of all ages, including infants, in immediate need of both fostering and adoption.

The more difficult question arises if you are European American, but are open to adopting a child of another racial or cultural heritage. Some people within the adoption field feel that transracial adoption should not be allowed or should be allowed only as a last resort. Others, however, feel the practice offers hope for many children in immediate need of families. There are strong and valid concerns on both sides of the issue.

The main argument for allowing transracial adoptions is easily stated and initially may seem compelling in itself. If transracial adoption is not allowed, many people believe, there is a strong probability that many children from minority backgrounds will never be adopted. Cultural identity is important as an ideal, but a child needs a family—transracial or not. Although minority families do adopt, formally and informally, at rates as high as or higher than white families, there simply may not be enough to provide permanent families to the many minority children now needing families.

The arguments against transracial adoption are more complex, but once understood, they also raise strong concerns. First, the focus on numbers alone may be superficial, or at least too narrow. Instead of asking whether white families should be allowed to adopt black children, we should ask what we can do to enable more children from a range of cultural groups to safely stay with their families—or at least to be adopted by relatives, neighbors, or others from their own cultural group. We should concentrate on addressing problems such as racism, poverty, and drug abuse, which lead to so many family disruptions. We should also work harder to recruit minority families to foster parent or adopt children, and avoid letting any factors be a barrier that could discriminate against minority families, such as adequacy of home or marital status.

It is also worth noting that many children who are adopted internationally come from countries (such as Korea, or some Latin American nations) where U.S. military or economic policies have at least arguably helped create enormous social upheaval and dislocation. At some point, we have to ask ourselves whether we are adopting the children of families our society has helped to disrupt, rather than addressing the policies that lead to family disruptions.

Truth can be found in both arguments, and some positive changes are occurring. In recent years, thanks in part to activists within and outside the social service system, many state social services departments now put greater and more imaginative effort into both helping biological families, and recruiting and supporting more minority adopters and foster parents. Proposed federal legislation aimed at funding appropriate services to prevent family breakup, such as the proposed Family Preservation Act, if passed, will likely be a big help.

At the same time, in practical recognition of the large numbers of minority children in immediate need of caring families, children are often placed transracially when enough matching placements cannot be found. Transracial foster parenting, never as controversial as adoption, remains common in most areas and is generally well accepted.

Adoption policies are not uniform. International adoption is often transracial, with European Americans commonly adopting Asian or Latin American Indian children. Many state and private agencies placing U.S. children for adoption, however, may require a racial match, or may delay adoption for months seeking such a match. Even agencies with aggressive racial-matching policies in adoptions, however, may make an exception if the prospective adopters are the child's current or former foster parents and the adoption appears to be in the child's best interest.

The decision whether or not to adopt a child of another race is difficult, particularly when ties of affection already exist. At a minimum, the decision should be made carefully, with full respect for the child's family and culture. If the child is old enough to understand the decision, the child's wishes should be a major, if not the major, consideration. Whatever the child's age, the possible difficulties should be considered, as well as possible benefits. It is important to give careful thought to the child's other possible options—including any you can help realize, such as providing foster care while cooperating with the agency's efforts to find the best adoptive home. Transracial adoption should never be undertaken to prove a point or to prove one's open-mindedness, because that places the adult's needs above the child's.

All that said, many happy interracial and intercultural families are created through adoption. In the most successful adoptions involving a racial or cultural mix, the family becomes, defines itself, and lives as an interracial or intercultural family. Living as an interracial or intercultural family does not mean, for example, merely that white parents encourage their black child to attend church with a black coworker, a practice that splits the family and suggests that African American culture is of interest only to African Americans. A better example would be the family that, as a family, lives in an interracial community, has black as well as white friends, and regularly attends an interracial or primarily black church. It may be the adoptive parents who study Spanish and save for an extended vacation in Chile with their Chilean son, or the family that joins a Korean American friendship society, and supports, through correspondence and donations, the family services work of the agency in Korea that sent them their two daughters.

Interracial and intercultural family life is not always easy, particularly as children grow older, and particularly in a society that remains disappointingly segregated. Nonetheless, some families have found it enriching, and some interracially and interculturally adopted young people have found the experience satisfying.

How to Use This Book

In organizing this book, we have tried to follow as logical a progression as possible. This chapter focused on understanding the basic needs of children and what options are available. Chapter 2 explores making decisions in the context of your own needs, preferences, abilities, and limitations. Together they can help prepare you to evaluate the options available, weigh what is realistic, and make decisions about parenting.

The next three chapters describe the basic options available: child and family mentoring (Chapter 3), foster parenting (Chapter 4), and adoption (Chapter 5). Each discusses children of all ages, of a variety of cultures, and with and without serious physical or emotional challenges. Each also describes options that are immediately available, at little or no cost. (As discussed in the chapters, however, not every type of child needing every type of parenting is immediately available without significant cost.)

Note that, in reading the chapters, you'll move from the most time-limited to the most time-intensive form of commitment. That is, child and family mentoring requires a part-time commitment, similar to a caring aunt, uncle, or grandparent; foster parenting requires full-time but temporary parenting; and adoption involves full-time, permanent parenting. At the same time, the chapters also happen to be ordered from the option needed by the greatest number of children (mentoring) to that needed by a smaller number (adoption). Sometimes, as you'll see, mentoring may lead to fostering, or fostering to adoption—much as dating sometimes leads to living together, or living together to marriage.

The final chapters explore specialized options, each of which has provided happy solutions for many families, although they may not be practical or available in all cases. Chapter 6 discusses the process through which a child is adopted by his or her former foster parent(s). International adoption, in Chapter 7, involves the adoption of children from other countries. Identified adoption, in Chapter 8, generally involves a person-to-person agreement between a birthmother and the adopters, leading to the adoption of an infant. Chapter 9 describes what is known as kinship care, when a relative, mentor, or family friend becomes that child's foster parent and may eventually adopt the child or become the child's permanent guardian.

We suggest that you read the first five chapters in order, even if you already feel strongly oriented toward one particular option. They lay out all of your options and are designed to give you a sense of the growing needs of children over time. After all, you may adopt a child, but one who was formerly in foster care. Or you may foster parent and help prepare some children for later adoption. Reading all the chapters will help you to gain a fuller picture of the child who will enter your life, as well as widen your horizons in terms of choices available.

After the first five chapters, feel free to skip around in the order of your interest. For the fullest view of your options, you'll want to read all the remaining chapters, but you are welcome to read selectively if you prefer.

Taking the First Step

As you read about the paths available to you, keep in mind that you never need tread them alone. Many others within your own community are struggling with the same decisions that you are, or have struggled and succeeded in building a life rich with children. Support groups—such as infertility groups, foster parent associations, adoption support and information exchanges, and other community groups—can offer much of the emotional nurturance and practical information you need. To find them, you can start with the national networks listed in the appendix of this book, or check the classified listings in your local community events papers. Staff at local mental health centers, state departments of social services, and adoption agencies also may know of groups in your community.

At the same time, continue to put energy into your personal friendships, your ability to nurture yourself, and your capacity to find peace and contentment in your life. This is important if you are part of a couple, and doubly important if you are single. Children bring joy, but they also bring heartache and frustration. And children who have been through trauma—which includes most children needing adoption or fostering today—can be especially challenging.

The child or children you adopt or foster parent may love you and need you, but healthy adult friends are more likely to consistently show you friendship and appreciation. The fuller your life is before you bring a child into it, the happier and more manageable it will be when the child—and the challenges—arrive.

All that said, you are indeed embarking on a wonderful adventure. There is a child waiting for you, a child with a history and a personality and a culture, and perhaps a lively spark of fun. You will change that child's life, and he or she will change yours. And, bit by bit, as you build the bonds of family and of relationship, your lives will be the richer for it.

Two

Making Decisions about Parenting

Decisions about parenting are among the most intimate, the most important, and the most challenging we ever make. If we're going to be able to meet the needs of children, we need to also have a sense of how our own needs will be met.

—Clarice Walker
District of Columbia Department of Human Services

Once you bring children into your life, their needs will and must eclipse your own. This is true in all families, however formed. Simply stated, kids have an incredible number of needs, and adults have a responsibility to provide for them. For many parents, there are months, and even years, when the sacrifices seem to outweigh the pleasures. So although parenting definitely has its joys and rewards, day-to-day fairness is not one of them.

In many adoptive and foster families, the neediness of

children, and the resulting responsibilities of adoptive and foster parents, tend to be greater than in biological families. There are several ways to address this. Extended family, friends, trusted babysitters, an adoptive or foster parent support group, and, if needed, child and family therapy all may offer crucial support. A sense of faith, and a sense of humor, may bring serenity in even the toughest times.

Yet planning for success, by making careful decisions up front, is also important. As much as possible, recognize and understand your own needs, desires, strengths, and interests—and then choose a lifestyle and type of child-raising that maximize that personal outlook. That way, the children may still be needy, but their needs and personalities will form a rough match with your own strengths and interests. The children's needs may still be a challenge, but fulfilling those needs will more likely bring you a sense of pride and satisfaction.

For example, suppose you were, as a child, a bright kid whose intelligence was never fully recognized or encouraged by the adults around you. You might gain special satisfaction in parenting a child who, due to emotional problems, has failed to work up to capacity in school. On the other hand, you might care more about warmth and affection than academic ability in children or adults. In that case, you might have a great deal to offer an affectionate six-year-old with Down's syndrome. If you are politically active and committed around AIDS issues, you might find extra meaning in caring for a child who is HIV-positive.

In each of these examples, the child's needs are great and could be daunting. Yet the parent can give more to the child, with the greatest degree of satisfaction, because the child's needs fit well with the parent's own interests and abilities.

Identifying Your Needs and Preferences

Each section in this chapter discusses a common area of concern among many adults who love children and want to build a family. As you read each, try to evaluate whether it describes a basic need in you, without which you simply couldn't be happy or satisfied, or merely something you'd prefer. Most people find that, in alternate parenting (as well as much of life), they can fulfill most or all of their needs but probably not all of their preferences.

For most of us, although we often fail to make the distinction, there is a great difference between what we want and what we need. I may *want* a certain fascinating, highly paid job I see advertised, but all I really *need*, for my welfare and self-esteem, is work that is satisfying and puts food on the table. I may *want* a spouse, friends, or a child with certain specific, highly attractive qualities, but what I *need* is loving relationships built on dignity and respect.

The more we can make this kind of distinction, particularly in a highly personal and often unpredictable area such as parenting, the more likely we are to have our basic needs met. We are also less likely to spin our wheels in frustration, looking for imagined perfection but overlooking real opportunities to enjoy and share happiness.

The Desire to Nurture

The desire to nurture, to feel a part of the never-ending cycle of growing and helping young life to grow, is one of life's most basic urges. Although the raising of young is common to all animals, humans are unusual in the length of time we spend with our young. For most animals, raising young to self-sufficiency means a time investment of perhaps a season, a year, or at most a few years. For humans, eighteen years is assumed, and may not even be the end. If we consider not only actual caregiving time but the years that the parental influence lingers, human parenting can be a lifetime proposition.

For this reason, and because of cultural and societal traditions, we spend most of our lives in a web of relationships designed to nurture and sustain us and others. We may be at once adult child, sibling, grandchild, and parent or foster parent—not to mention spouse, employee, friend, and community member. The urge to nurture, which may well be a part of our basic biological nature, is daily reinforced by the habits and traditions that surround us.

Many of us experience the urge to nurture not as a mere preference or desire but as an actual need. This perception is almost certainly accurate. Just as individual human life is preserved through instinctual sensations (for example, hunger propels us to eat, and cold urges us to protect our bodies), so is human life in general preserved through instinctual urges. Sexual desire propels many to procreate, and the need to nurture allows us to protect, preserve, and guide the young lives thus created.

The means of expressing and fulfilling the need to nurture, however, may differ greatly among individuals. Nature would have done a sorry job of protecting the human race if the need to nurture had been imprinted into our instincts only as a narrowly defined urge to parent babies or children personally raised by one or two persons from infancy to adulthood. Throughout history parents have died or become unable to care for their children, requiring others to step in. Nurturance is needed by and (although in different ways) can be expressed with children and adolescents of all ages.

Certainly, the traditional and most common means of fulfilling the need to nurture has always been to have a baby (or, over time, several) and, if possible, raise the child or children to adulthood. Because that tradition is so pervasive, we may automatically, without even realizing it, think of it as if it were identical with the need to nurture.

A Personal Exploration

As you examine your own need to nurture, try to clear your mind of preconceptions you may have as to how you'll fulfill that need. This can be difficult, for it can mean putting aside a lifetime of assumptions. It also, like any creative thinking, may mean setting aside social expectations and the comfort of following the path that your own parents and many of your friends may have followed.

You may also have to face real grief in letting go of past dreams that are no longer realistic for you. If, for example, you and your partner have tried unsuccessfully to conceive, perhaps even tried surgical intervention, you have experienced a serious and painful loss of an important shared dream. For many people, the idea of adoption may provide a short-term escape from the painful feelings associated with the loss of the dream of childbirth. The imagined adoptive child replaces the imagined birthchild in their minds, offering comfort and a new focus for their emotional energy.

If you have allowed yourself to grieve for the child who will not be born to you, redirecting your thoughts to a child you can parent is a healthy and constructive adaptation. If unacknowledged feelings remain buried, however, those feelings can lend a painful urgency to the process. They could even, in some cases, strain the relationship with the child adopted.

You may, for example, feel a strong, almost overpowering insistence that your adoptive experience must be as much like the imagined birth experience as possible: the child must be a baby, must look as much like you and your partner as possible, must be perfectly healthy, must be legally guaranteed to be yours from day one, must have no future contact with the birthmother, and so on. This line of thinking, although completely understandable, is almost certain to lead to disappointment. No adoption—and, in fact, few births—can be so predictable and controllable. Children turn out to look or act differently from their parents, to have possibly serious health difficulties, and to develop emotional ties to adults other than the parents who raise them. You may also, for practical or even financial reasons, have difficulty adopting a newborn.

Anxiety over a child's name also can be an example of a deeply felt but unrecognized need to simulate the birth experience. Most people do give their child, on adoption, their own family surname; except in the case of a teen or older child who does not want his or her last name changed, this is a sensible and appropriate way to declare a new family bond. The child's given (or first) name, however, is personal. Most children older than infants already have a name when they are adopted. Even when as young as one year old, the child knows her or his given name and identifies with it. It is, as one perceptive adoptive mother noted, "about the only thing my son had to call his own." Considerable evidence—and common sense—suggest that changing the child's name is likely to add significantly to the child's sense of confusion and loss.

Despite this, many adoptive parents feel a strong desire to change, or at least modify, the given name of a child adopted between, say, age one and age four. If they don't understand that this can cause anxiety and pain for the child, some actually do change the name. The unconscious reason may be that the name is a reminder of a reality that is painful for the adopting parent to confront: that this child has a biological family, a history, and perhaps a distinct culture, quite separate and apart from the relationship with the adoptive family.

If realities such as these are highly distressing to you, you may need to take a step back and nurture yourself. Foster and adoptive parenting have special joys all their own, but they are different paths from parenting through birth. If you have lost the dream of birthparenting, you need to grieve that loss, through tears, talks with friends, and possibly some therapy, before you can begin to see your current options in a more realistic light. Only then can you truly be free to explore the paths open to you.

Assessing Your Interests and Talents

Once you have, as much as possible, cleared the slate of stereotypes and assumptions, ask yourself simple, direct questions about what types of parenting relationship you could enjoy, and what types of children you could parent well. These questions might include, for example, the following:

- What ages of children do you most enjoy?
- What are your greatest talents in caring for children?
- If you had to choose between a highly dependent or a highly independent child, which would you choose?
- Could you love a child, knowing you might have to let him or her go if that were best for the child?
- Cost considerations aside, would you prefer the intensity of a permanent intimate relationship with one child, or the happy hubbub of a home filled with children?

Brainstorming along these lines, personally or with a partner, can help you imagine a family structure that fits your needs and evaluate the options in the chapters that follow.

Every form of involvement with children discussed in this book can fulfill the need to nurture—and at least one of those routes is almost certain to be available to you. So you know it is within your power to fulfill the most basic *need* driving you.

You may also be able to exercise many of your *preferences* in expressing or fulfilling that need. For example, if you adore babies and feel you have a special gift with them, you might consider specialized foster parenting of infants and toddlers. If you have a talent with teenagers, you might literally change the direction of a young person's life by foster parenting a teenager or serving as a mentor to a teen parent. If you most prefer to offer nurturance in a single relationship over a period of years, adoption of a young child might be most attractive to you. Whichever route you choose, you'll have a chance to show your affection, watch children change and grow, and know that you have helped to enrich their lives.

The Sense That Your Love Will Be Rewarded and Returned

Although parenting requires one to offer a child love and caring without regard to whether it is returned, most of us hope deep down that our love will be rewarded. We like to imagine a lifetime friendship with our children, lasting into the years when they have children of their own.

For some people, the idea of foster parenting, and even adoption of an older child, seems hollow. They can't imagine that it is really family, that the relationships could have the depth and meaning and longevity of biological family ties, or of adoption from birth.

The truth is that there are no guarantees in parenting—period. Many biological parents, after eighteen years of raising and loving a child, see that child move to another state, become busy with career or other responsibilities, become emotionally estranged, or even die. And, conversely, many foster parents, having accepted from the outset that they will love their foster children expecting to let them go, are happily surprised to find that at least a few of those former foster children have become lifetime friends.

To some degree, the meaningfulness of your relationships may have more to do with what you put into them than with their legal or biological basis. Yet it is also true in parenting, and particularly in adoption and foster parenting, that you must be willing to offer your affection and caring to a child without expecting the child to give back immediately.

When a child comes into your home, you can and should expect and require reasonable obedience to reasonable rules, nondestructiveness, and so on. Yet a child entering foster care, or an older child being adopted, may already be using all of his or her emotional energy just to cope with the life changes occurring. He or she probably will not be able to show affection quickly. (This is not always true; some children are quite affectionate right from the start.)

The reserved child actually may be showing healthy instincts. A child who offers love too freely may be hurt again and again; a child who expresses constant appreciation for being cared for may be showing that he or she doesn't feel worthy of being so loved. Conversely, a child who does not quickly respond with intimacy and devotion to a new parent figure may be honoring his or her relationship with the birthparent. By not requiring a quick show of love and appreciation, you offer the child a gift that should not be rare, but is: the chance just to be a kid, and to be cared for as a kid, without regard to what he or she can offer in return.

Can this apparently unequal relationship be satisfying for the foster parent, or the new adoptive parent, as well? Surprisingly enough, the answer seems to be a resounding yes. If you have ever listened to new parents rhapsodize over the joys of their new baby (while a part of you said to yourself, But seriously, now, that kid keeps squalling, can't even talk, and you can't get a decent night's sleep), you have an idea of what it is like to hear many long-term foster and adoptive parents. The joy in making a difference, in giving to a child and watching that child grow and gain confidence, is unlike any other.

As for comfort and companionship in your old age, it's

hard to predict. If you raise one or a few children from infancy, you'll have a few well-tended eggs in one carefully constructed basket. If you spend an equal number of years as a foster parent, with children coming and going over those years, you'll have more eggs and less elaborate baskets. Neither is a guarantee, but ultimately, the best you can do is simply to love the children in your life and let them go. If you have done your job well—and are fortunate—they'll become independent but also choose to maintain a close relationship.

Your ongoing need to feel loved and respected as a person, however—as opposed to your desire to have any one child show love and gratitude to you on any given day—is absolutely valid. It is all too easy, in parenting in general, and perhaps in foster and adoptive parenting in particular, to fall prey to social expectations that you should give selflessly and endlessly, without needing or requiring nurturance yourself.

To avoid this, you'll have to seek nurturance and practical help from those who *can* give it to you, such as your partner, your friends, good day care, and other social services. We'll also explore later in the book the services available, often free of charge, from the state social services department when you are adopting or fostering a child with special needs.

The Desire to Be Part of a Larger Community

∽

One of the great joys of childraising is the way children can help make us part of a larger community. Teachers, neighbors, and parents of other children all may seem more accessible when the connection is made through a child. Perhaps the most classic example of this was in the post–World War II baby-boom towns such as Levittown, New York, built specifically as communities for the young families of ex-GIs. After a few years, it seemed as if every family that did not have a two- and a four-year-old had a one- and a three-year-old. Community ties formed almost automatically: "Bring your kids over Saturday, and we'll bring ours to your house on Sunday."

It is helpful to think of such a clearcut example of a community based on highly similar families, precisely because so much has changed. Today traditional families of married parents with two or more children born to them represent only a small percentage of U.S. families. Single parents, divorced parents, second marriage families, and adoptive and foster families all abound. Even among ostensibly traditional families, changing work and economic patterns mean that old-style community ties don't happen without effort. The rare mother who can take her child to the park on weekday afternoons probably will not find half a dozen other mothers there with their children. The Saturday afternoon father-son softball game, if it still exists, doubtless must be scheduled well in advance. This means that all families must make an extra effort if they are to be part of a larger community of families.

People considering adoption or foster parenting commonly fear that the choice will put them out of the mainstream, making it harder to be part of the community around them. In reality, however, this is usually not the case, and certainly doesn't have to be. First, you'll probably find that kids are kids, and you'll be talking with teachers and neighbors and parents of friends just the same as any other parent. You may face the occasional insensitive remark, but you are unlikely to be ostracized.

Even so, your family probably will have interests and concerns particular to adoption or fostering, and may well want to connect with others with similar concerns. You can become a part of a specialized community in a classically American way: join a group. While some of your neighbors go to a Lamaze class, and others a parent stress support group, you can join a foster or adoptive parent support and friendship group, or perhaps sign up for a class in fostering teens or fostering children who've been abused.

Again, without question, your *need* to be part of a larger community around you can be fulfilled in the context of any form of fostering or adoption discussed in this book. Your *preferences* as to what kind of community involvement you enjoy most may influence the choice you see as most favorable.

If you are very outgoing and enjoy meeting new people, for example, foster parenting might be an excellent choice. Because part of the foster care process is to help preserve and improve the relationships already important in the foster child's life, you will probably be asked to interact with a number of others involved with the children in your care. These may include the child's medical providers, teachers, perhaps a counselor, the family social worker, and, if appropriate, other family members. Depending on the policies in your area (and local foster parent groups can influence these policies), you may be treated as a valued member of a child welfare team.

Adoption does not ordinarily involve this same level of ongoing involvement with the system. It may, however, heighten your opportunities for continuity of friendships of the "Let's take your Johnny and my Jimmy to the zoo" variety. So if your sense of community is very much connected with nesting and settling in, adoption might be a better choice for you.

Your decision to adopt or foster parent may also affect your choice of where to live. If you plan to foster parent, for example, you may want to consider a racially and culturally diverse community where almost any child would feel comfortable. Similarly, adoptive parents of children with special needs often choose, and sometimes deliberately relocate to, communities with good special education programs and/or good medical care and social services.

The Desire for Privacy

Most of us appreciate a certain level of privacy in our lives. Although probably not an ingrained human need (in many societies, people live their entire lives with little or no privacy), it is certainly a strong preference for many. In the United States, which has always valued individualism, the desire for privacy may be especially strong. We also tend to be especially sensitive to issues of privacy if we feel we are being judged.

For many people, loss of privacy, particularly during the application process, is one of the major frustrations of foster or adoptive parenting. You'll be opening your home and your life to a certain amount of scrutiny, and you may feel invaded.

You can take several concrete steps if loss of privacy is a concern for you. The first is gaining knowledge and understanding. As intrusive as the interview and approval process may feel to you, it really is necessary for the child's protection.

Try thinking of it this way. If someone gave you the

responsibility of finding a home for a child, would you feel comfortable handing that child over to someone you had just met, without finding out quite a bit more about that person? True, nature gives babies to people every day without conducting interviews, but would that make you feel comfortable doing less than your best to find a loving family for that particular child? And, if you had hundreds of such children to place, wouldn't you worry about the dangers of letting it be widely known that the children were available to any apparently respectable person who asked? The process might be simplified for nice people like you, but what if less nice people used the opportunity to exploit children? Or suppose even well-meaning people ended up with children whose needs were totally mismatched to the adoptive parent's abilities. In this light, it is easier to see the loss of privacy not as a personal insult but as one of the many sacrifices a parent must make out of love for a child or for children in general.

A second step is to use interviews as a two-way street for you to gain information about the agency, the process, and the child or children you may foster or adopt. Preadoption interviews ten or twenty years ago may have been designed just to decide if the candidates would be good parents, but the role today is much more subtle.

Children available for foster care and adoption today are as varied in their individual qualities as are prospective parents. The goal of the interviews, therefore, is not so much to determine if the prospective parents are "good enough" but to explore whether a positive and healthy match exists. Any decisions made must be mutual, between you, the agency, and, if old enough to participate in the decision, the child. If you see and use the interviews in this way, they'll seem less an invasion of your privacy and more a mutual sharing of information.

Your choice of route to follow in building your family may also have an impact on how much and in what way your privacy is affected. If you choose adoption, particularly of an infant, you'll probably face a more in-depth interview process initially, and a tapering off of any required contacts with the agency after the adoption is complete. (They should still remain available, however, as a resource if needed.)

If you choose foster parenting, adoption of an older child or a child with special needs, or adoption of a sibling group, you will probably find the initial application process to be more streamlined than with adoption of an infant. The reason for this is simple: since foster and adoptive parents are desperately needed for these children, agency workers must make the process as attractive and accessible as possible.

As discussed in the section above, however, these situations—especially foster parenting—are also the ones in which continued agency contact, and contact with others in the child's life, will probably be necessary. Although the continued contact is generally not aimed at questioning or evaluating the foster parent, but rather exchanging information about the children, it does represent a less private family lifestyle. Once again, you have the choice whether to regard that contact as an intrusion or to turn it into an opportunity. The sooner you begin to think of the social worker bringing children into your care as a colleague, not an authority figure, the more comfortable you'll probably feel.

The Need for Acceptance

Sometimes the concerns we have about family privacy are as much practical as emotional. If your lifestyle differs from the standard norm for traditional adoption (that is, you are not an upper-middle-class, married, heterosexual couple in your mid-twenties to late thirties), you may fear that you'll be judged unfairly and disqualified through the application process.

Although policies among agencies arranging adoption and foster parenting vary widely, some generalizations may be made. Old prejudices about who makes "good" parents die hard, just as do old prejudices about who makes an "ideal" child. If you want to adopt or foster a child with special needs, an older child, or a sibling group, you can probably find a local agency that will not adhere to traditional stereotypes—if not out of progressiveness, then simply because you are offering a stable family life to a child or children who might otherwise not find one. If you insist on a child considered by some to be the "traditional ideal adoptee" (that is, a white baby without identified health problems), you might face a requirement that you be equally stereotypical.

If this is your situation, are you being unfairly restricted and compartmentalized in your choices? Absolutely. There is no reason to assume, for example, that a loving single parent or a gay couple can't provide a caring home for an infant. There may be challenges, but these would apply at least equally to caring for a special needs child or sibling group. You may also have unusual strengths to offer.

Yet consider this: The inherent value system, which implies that a certain type of parent is "better," is even more disturbing insofar as it implies that a certain type of child is "better." You can make the most powerful personal statement against this type of prejudice by seeking to build a strong, loving family with a child or children who is as unfairly shut out by stereotypes as you may be. You may also have something unique to offer that child: an understanding of what it is like to be different from the crowd, and an example of strength and pride in being who you are.

You may find that foster parenting offers you wider opportunities than adoption. In most states, age, marital status, and economic status are not barriers to foster parenting provided the applicant is adult, caring, and financially and physically self-sufficient. This is in part due to the great need for foster parents, and in part due to the perception that children in transition have less of a need for a traditionally defined home life. Many single and older people, in particular, have long records as excellent foster parents.

Prejudices against gay couples persist in many states, both in adoption and in foster care, but policies are very much in flux. Oddly, gays may be allowed in some areas to adopt, but not foster parent; in other areas, they may foster parent but not adopt. In many cases, discrepancies may result more from political pressure and legal concerns than from any informed view as to what benefits children. Where no specific policy exists, individual social workers may routinely work with gay foster parents. A social worker who gets to know and respect you can be an important ally, even if agency barriers exist.

If you have concerns about possible agency prejudices based on your lifestyle, age, or marital status, try to learn as much as possible about agency policies before you officially apply to foster parent or adopt—and then focus on agencies that appear to have the most inclusive policies. Simply calling and asking agency requirements, or asking to have written materials sent to you, may be a good starting point. You can also learn a great deal about local agency policies, and perhaps have an impact on them, by joining adoptive or foster parent networks in your state.

Self-assessment

Occasionally, concerns about the screening process are based not on fear of prejudice but on actual concerns about one's own suitability. If you have traits or tendencies that could lead you to abuse or neglect a child, you should steer clear of any form of foster or adoptive parenting, or any private time with a child—even if your intentions are positive.

The most obvious reason, of course, is for the child's safety. Even if you think you have abusive urges under control, that control can break all too easily. Some children who were physically abused in the past may behave in infuriating ways, severely testing your self-control. Similarly, some children who were sexually abused in the past may have learned behaviors that, although a cry for help, may seem or be interpreted as sexually provocative.

It is also worth noting that children in foster care or who have been adopted tend to have an unusually high degree of contact with school counselors and the social service system. Any reabuse would almost certainly be revealed at some time, and punishments are severe.

Financial Concerns

For most families, costs are a concern. Many loving adults who would like to build a family don't have thousands or even hundreds of dollars to spend. Even for the financially comfortable, cost can be a factor. After all, every dollar spent on bringing a child into your family is money that could be spent directly on the child's needs and future opportunities.

Fortunately, cost need not be a barrier to building a fulfilling family life. Foster parenting, in fact, costs less than biological parenting. No fees are charged to foster parents, and training is free. Once a child or children are in your home, you will even receive a small stipend to help pay for their food and clothes. Medical costs will be billed not to you but to Medicaid or the state social services department.

Cost should also not be a barrier to adopting most older children, sibling groups, and/or children with special needs. Most state programs and some nonprofit agencies do not charge fees for adopting these children. You may even be able to obtain an adoption subsidy to cover ongoing medical and other expenses. As in foster parenting, the subsidies generally will not exceed, and may not even meet, actual costs, but they can prevent costs from becoming a problem.

One type of adoption, however, is usually very expensive—the adoption of a European American or an internationally adopted infant without identified health problems. The high cost is unfortunate and offensive for several reasons: it may restrict the adoption of some children to only those who can afford the fee; it may impose a hardship on an adoptive family at the very time it should be supported; and it seems almost to suggest a ranking system that values some children above others. Many in the field have urged greater public funding and regulation to avoid this, but so far the practice remains.

There are cost differences based on type of adoption (with identified adoption or international adoption generally the more expensive methods), but it is rare to spend less than $5,000, and not uncommon to spend up to $20,000 or more.

Many factors will affect the actual fee, such as the agency chosen, whether a sliding fee scale is used, the cost of any services offered to the birthmother, and whether travel is involved.

If you choose this route, don't be afraid to ask for complete cost information up front and to make comparisons. The joy of a child is priceless—but an adoption agency, or a law firm assisting in an adoption, is just a group of people providing a service of specific and comparable value.

What to Do while You're Deciding, Applying, or Waiting for a Child

If you love children, don't wait to make them a part of your life. Right now, in your community, countless children need caring adult guidance. Why stay at home grieving the absence of a child in your life, while a child on your block is being turned away from, say, an after-school tutoring program because of a shortage of adult volunteers?

Although there are many reasons to procrastinate or avoid volunteering with children, you don't have to accept them—even if you hear yourself voicing them. You may think you are too busy, but if you are too busy to offer a few hours a week, you are certainly too busy to become a parent. You may try it and find that it is fun but quite a bit of work, and the staff where you volunteer doesn't show much appreciation. Hmmm . . . overworked and underappreciated—sounds a lot like parenting.

Volunteering with children may help you clarify, broaden, or redirect your long-range goals. It may also help build self-confidence in reaching those goals and strengthen your application to adopt or foster parent.

Perhaps the most common hesitation for an adult longing to become a parent is the fear that being around children will be too emotionally upsetting, serving as a constant reminder of the uncompleted family. The experiences of those who try volunteering, however, tend to prove the fear unfounded. Children have a way of drawing our attention from ourselves and our troubles—and the nurturing relationships that develop are often satisfying in themselves.

Three

Child and Family Mentoring

If there's a child in your community who doesn't have a parent, or doesn't have stability, make a commitment. Not everyone can be a foster parent or an adoptive parent, and not everyone should be. But everyone should make a commitment to a child. Children need that; black, white, blue, or gray, they need to know there's an adult who really cares, who is committed to them. And there are too many children today who don't get that feeling.

—Ken Johnson
District of Columbia Department of Human Services

In a child's eyes, commitment is not measured by your age, your health, your marital status, or your lifestyle. Commitment is communicated by how much you care, how constant you are in what you can provide, and the simple fact of unconditional affection. Yet, in the adult world, age, health, and other practical factors may influence what form of commitment to a child is most realistic. You may have a great deal to offer a child but be uncertain whether you can meet the daily responsibilities of adoptive or foster parenting.

Just as practical and emotional factors in your life may affect what you can offer, practical and emotional factors in the lives of children affect what they need. Although many children today need, temporarily or permanently, alternate parenting, far more need some level of supplemental parenting. That is, they need a caring adult who can offer guidance, friendship, and hope, not by replacing the child's existing family but by supplementing, expanding, and possibly even helping to strengthen it. This type of friendship can truly change a child's life, as well as, possibly, your own.

You probably are aware of, and may even be involved in, some of the many important and fulfilling ways to volunteer, or to work for pay, with children. Like many people, however, you may be searching for a way to develop a bond with children that creates a real sense of kinship, for the child and for you. You may feel that you'd make some child or children a wonderful grandparent, or uncle, or aunt—but your existing extended family, if any, lives far away. Or you may already be a wonderful and active grandparent, or uncle, or aunt, yet feel you have still more to give.

All children, like adults, need a sense of community and kinship with those around them—especially children whose parents are otherwise isolated and under stress. In this chapter, we'll explore some specific, much needed forms of relationship that can help create a sense of community and kinship with a child in need. Each involves not the full assumption of parental responsibilities but the supportive sharing of them, much as relatives may fulfill that role within an extended family. Yet each is a formal, defined role in the child's life, which may be initiated, like adoption or foster parenting, through a child and family service agency in your community.

Many people, of course, form kinship style ties informally with friends or neighbors, or through community or religious traditions such as godparenting. That is a valid option but, like conventional volunteering, probably not one you need a lot of guidance to pursue.

You may also be interested in reaching the children most in need—building relationships that will have a real impact—and that is what this chapter can help you do. Consider that, for example, to a relatively stable family new to your church, you may be a welcome friendly face. But to a teenage mother who has dropped out of school (and never went to church), and to her infant child, your friendship just may be a lifeline.

The options we'll explore in this chapter, although quite different from adoption or even foster parenting, may nonetheless be deep and meaningful for everyone involved. They also have their own significant challenges.

Becoming a Mentor

Children and family have always been at the center of Jane Thomas's life. She and her husband, Randy, raised five children, and were happy to do so. They've always said that, despite the challenges and frustrations, they'd do it all over again.

Well, in theory anyway. In practice, Randy is happy devoting his retirement years to writing and carpentry, and Jane is happy with a mix of activities that includes children, but not full-time. Yet, given Jane's obvious warmth, experience, and rapport with the children in her life, the less-than-full-time hours clearly translate into round-the-clock caring.

"I started getting involved with young children again so I'd get out of my grown children's hair," she explains, laughing. "I'd bite my tongue to stay quiet, then slip and hear myself hinting to my older married daughter about how nice a grandchild would be. Then my youngest, who was just a teenager at the time, would say 'Sure, Mom, I'll make you a grandchild.' She was just teasing (I think), but it sure stopped me up short. I said to myself, I better get myself some 'pretend' grandchildren soon or we're all in trouble."

Jane's first involvement was—for the second time—acting as a Cub Scout den mother. "I met the scoutmaster, and he asked me, 'And how old is your little boy, Mrs. Thomas?' 'Twenty-three,' I said. Although I laughed, I was shocked at how shocked he seemed. He couldn't seem to understand why a sane adult would willingly spend time with children, unless their 'own' child was in the group.

"That seemed sad to me, and wrong. Here we are, a nation of basically good-hearted folks, with the resources to make life better for the children in our communities—but it doesn't always happen, because we're only worrying about our 'own' children."

Over the next several years, Jane kept up her involvement with children in a variety of ways: joining a tutoring program, teaching Sunday school, helping to organize a local Special Olympics for children with disabilities, and leading a story group at the local public library.

Then a newspaper article about a program within her community, the Baltimore Child Abuse Prevention Center, led her to broaden her commitment. The program was looking for volunteers who could serve as mentors to parents (usually single mothers) who felt overwhelmed and isolated, and feared they might abuse or neglect their children. Jane remembered her own difficult times as a young mother: when their first child was born shortly after Randy was shipped overseas during World War II; when they had a houseful ranging from age three to thirteen, and Randy lost his job; when the older children hit their teens smack in the middle of the 1960s drug culture. Jane knew she wouldn't have any easy answers to offer a stress-ridden young mother today, but she knew she could at least offer friendship and understanding, and perhaps some regular babysitting.

The program offered volunteers special training and help in setting limits, as well as services to the children and families involved. Thanks to its comprehensive, interpersonal approach, it is one of the most effective programs known in helping to prevent child abuse, family breakup, or foster care placement.

Today Jane counts her experiences with the families she's come to know through the program as among the most meaningful in her life. She is still close with the family she started with, having shared much of the childhood of two boys, Michael and Jerome, who were, when she met them, a three-year-old and an infant. Equally important, she has watched—and she hopes helped—their mother, Marie, grow in confidence, strength, and tenderness.

"My own mother died when I was twelve," Jane says quietly, "and in some ways I never realized what I'd lost until I'd shared that type of bond with Marie, from the other side. I wanted grandchildren, Marie needed a motherly type of friend, and Mikey and Jerome needed grandmotherly affection. It couldn't have worked better."

Incidentally, Jane's adult children did eventually begin having children, who are also an important part of Jane's life. Yet the friendship with Marie and Michael and Jerome remains strong—and Jane has recently begun mentoring another young family as well.

"I still see Mikey and Jerome more often than some of my grandchildren, who live in other states," says Jane. "At this point, I hardly distinguish—all of them feel like family to me."

Why Child and Family Mentoring Is Important

The role that Jane Thomas fulfills in the life of Mikey, Jerome, and their mother is commonly known as child and family mentoring, although other names may be used, such as parent partnering, youth and family counselor, lay therapist, or, in programs involving mostly senior citizens, foster grandparenting. The mentor role is designed to echo the way a healthy extended family works, creating a kinship network among the children, their family, and an additional caring adult.

For several reasons, the extended family serves as a good model in thinking about a meaningful relationship with a child. The extended family is, of course, a long-cherished tradition, in our culture as well as others. It has offered strength and a sense of belonging to countless children and parents, in much the way the parent-child bond itself has. For children, who deeply need a sense of security, but whose own parents alone may be unable to offer them sufficient stability, child and family mentoring can play an invaluable role.

Because child and family mentoring involves the child's parent as well as the child, it is more likely to survive and grow over time than other relationships the child may have. If you volunteer with a local kindergarten class, the children will move on each year; you'll wave happily in the halls, and some will stop by to say hello, but that may be it. If you become a mentor to a young family in crisis, however, you may well stay close for years, because you are a help and support to the children *within* the family context. This continuity over time is enriching and meaningful for the adults involved, and is a crucial boost to the child's sense of security and confidence.

Finally, child and family mentoring can help affirm and integrate the child's world. Today many economically and emotionally impoverished youngsters live in two worlds—the parental home, and the "real world" of school, after-school programs, health care center, and so on. If the parent is never involved in any way in the child's wider world, the schism between the two may grow wider and wider. The child may pick up a message that the parent is "out of it," a source not of strength but of shame. At the same time, the parent may grow distrustful of the child's world and may lose confidence as a parent. Since the child's sense of identity is so heavily dependent on the parent, the child may suffer a loss of self-esteem as well. It is not easy to break through this isolation, but a committed friendship, in which an adult from the child's wider world demonstrates friendly respect to the child's parent, can help enormously to bridge the gap.

The Role of Respect

An important part of Jane's friendship with Marie and her children was mutual respect. Marie respected Jane's experience and her willingness to share it; Jane respected Marie's commitment to her children, and her willingness to ask for and accept help. That respect helped them to share their concern and affection for the children, and formed the seeds of eventual friendship.

If you share your life with a child, you may or may not become close friends with the child's parents as well. It is crucial, however, to cultivate and communicate respect: for the child, the parent, and the child's culture and community. At the same time, it is also healthy to communicate a pride in yourself and your community, and to encourage the child and the child's family to share and enjoy differences.

Despite the obvious importance of mutual respect, it is not always easy to develop and maintain. Indeed, for some, it is the most challenging aspect of any form of child and family mentoring, in part because the neediest children generally have parents under the most stress. The same anger or hurt or depression that is so heart-wrenching in a child may be expressed in unattractive ways by the child's parent. It is important to remember that the parent was once a child—quite possibly one with many unmet needs—who is now trying, however imperfectly, to do better for her or his child.

If the parent seems distrustful of you, also consider that she or he may have had bad experiences in the past with people who promised to help but didn't follow through. Trust will come with time, as you show yourself to be caring and dependable.

Another part of the challenge of developing mutual respect may be our own fears and prejudices. Most of us tend to make friends with those who are outwardly similar to us, in age, culture, education, income level, interests, and style of communication. Child and family mentoring, in many cases, asks us to grow beyond that.

When we do begin to develop empathy and respect, we

often see, as Jane did in Marie, surprising strengths and gifts in even the most stress-ridden families. For some, this expanded vision is a moving and unexpected benefit of the mentoring process.

A good mentoring program will have training and staff supports that will help you understand your role and the needs and strengths of the child and the family. It should also be available to provide you with help and guidance in meeting any challenges that arise.

A Growing Commitment

In general, child and family mentoring involves a long-term commitment, but for a limited amount of time per week. Sometimes, however, if the child needs it and the mentoring adult is willing and able, that commitment may grow over time.

The experience of Gary Williams is a good example. Gary, a jeweler by trade, began thinking about the absence of children in his life the year he turned thirty. A gay man, happily settled in a long-term, committed relationship with his partner, Tom, he remembered his own teen and preteen years with a great deal of pain. One day, sitting in a city park, he heard two boys, age eleven or twelve, calling another boy a "fag." He didn't intervene, for fear it would only bring the child more taunts later, but it hurt to watch and do nothing.

Gay teens, Gary knew, face significant social ostracism, and are more likely than heterosexuals to experience depression, emotional disturbances, and even suicide attempts. Gary had struggled with self-esteem issues as a young man, and had been helped by friends and a good therapist. It was time, he decided, to give back.

Gary called a local residential treatment center for emotionally disturbed youths and made an appointment with a volunteer coordinator there. Meeting with the coordinator, he discussed his interest. He'd like to volunteer at the center, helping however he could. Possibly, he said, his own perspective as someone who has struggled with issues of acceptance and self-esteem, and who is now settled and happy, would provide comfort and hope to some young people.

The coordinator told Gary about the center's recreation counselor program, in which a volunteer takes on a "big brother" role with a youth in the program, sharing in recreational activities and helping with schoolwork. For youths who have difficulty meeting with their parents during family visits, the youth counselor may help to bridge the gap, leading an informal activity that involves both parents and children.

After some discussion, the counselor suggested that Gary might make a good recreation counselor to a fourteen-year-old resident of the program named Hector. Quiet and outwardly somewhat sullen, Hector had been deeply hurt by his father's rejection, and what he saw as his mother's failure to stand by him, when the family learned he was gay. He had been admitted to the center with severe depression four months before, and had been improving slowly. As the only openly gay youth in the program, he remained isolated.

The recreation counselor program involved a six-hour training program, and required a three-hours-a-week, one-year time commitment. Gary agreed, completed the training, and was introduced to Hector. Over the next year, Gary spent nearly every Saturday morning with Hector, playing pool, shooting baskets, or just talking. Despite Hector's initial distrust, he soon grew to like and respect Gary. He began confiding in Gary, finding they could talk comfortably about everything from family problems to AIDS prevention. Although Gary's partner, Tom, worked most Saturdays, he occasionally was able to join them. Hector liked Tom, too, and seemed encouraged to see a working, committed adult gay relationship.

At Hector's request, Gary made it a point to be there during some of the visits by Hector's family. In a way, this was the most challenging responsibility Gary had with Hector, because, in truth, he felt angry with Hector's parents on Hector's behalf. Nor did he expect a particularly warm reception from them, because they had been told from the outset that Hector's recreation counselor was gay. Determined to help Hector rebuild his bridges, however, Gary always treated Hector's mother with friendly respect. Hector's father never visited.

Fourteen months after Gary became Hector's recreation counselor, Hector's psychiatrist and a caseworker from the local department of social services met with Gary to discuss an important issue. Hector had improved dramatically over the past year, they all agreed, and the psychiatrist believed that he was nearly ready to leave the treatment center and reenter a family setting. Unfortunately, Hector would not be able to return home; his father violently opposed his return, and his mother felt she'd be unable to protect Hector or, for that matter, herself from the father's anger.

To the caseworker's surprise, Hector's mother had suggested Gary as a foster parent, since the family had no relatives nearby and Hector so clearly felt comfortable with Gary. The caseworker, after some thought, agreed that the choice would be a good one (particularly given the shortage of foster families willing to take a teen male with a history of emotional problems). Would Gary be willing, asked the caseworker, to become Hector's foster parent?

Gary's first reaction was fear. He had never raised a child, much less a teenager with emotional problems, and he'd never expected to have primary responsibility for one, even temporarily. He also was concerned that Hector would need continuing structure and mental health services, and lacked the ability to safely care for himself while Gary and Tom were at work. Yet, as he talked it over with Tom, he became more confident. Both of them had had younger siblings, and both felt committed to Hector. After confirming that Hector's case plan would include the hospital's outpatient after-school program as long as needed, Gary said yes.

Gary and Tom's status as a gay couple, incidentally, did not arise as a major issue, probably because the hospital staff already knew them and felt comfortable with their role in Hector's life. Regulations in their state for foster parents did not mention sexual orientation, and allowed either a married couple or a single person to become foster parents. (Other adult household members were also subject to a criminal record check but would not become official foster parents.) So Gary became Hector's foster father, and Tom the "other household member."

Hector lived with Gary and Tom for about six months. During that time, Hector's mother decided to separate from Hector's father, fleeing secretly to do so. Once she and the younger children were safely settled in a new community, Hector returned home. Hector went home with mixed feelings, but both he and his mother seemed to have learned from their experiences.

At the same time, the six months with Gary and Tom had cemented a lifetime friendship. As Hector put it, "Back in the hospital, I thought maybe Gary and Tom were just doing their good deed thing. After I stayed with them, I knew we were solid."

Finding the Right Opportunity

Although child development experts—and common wisdom—have long recognized the importance of extended-family-style caring in a child's life, the child welfare system has begun only recently to use it formally as a model for serving children and families under stress. You may find that the type of child and family mentoring program described here, although useful in almost any setting serving children of stress-ridden families, may not currently be a part of many child-based programs within your community. You may have to make several calls to a range of child and family service groups before you find opportunities similar to those described here.

Some national organizations can help you identify programs within your community that emphasize mentoring on an extended-family-style model, or even help you advocate or organize a local program if none exists. The National Resource Center on Family-Based Services is a leader in this area. It publishes a directory of programs offering a range of family-based services, which are indexed to show which use volunteers. Additionally, the Child Welfare League of America, the American Public Welfare Association, and the National Foster Parent Association all provide leadership in the effort to offer children community-based, parent-supportive options. All are listed in the appendix.

Many newspapers feature a volunteer opportunities column, which is a good way to learn about programs within your community. Your state social services department, and private family service and abuse prevention agencies, are also good sources. Your local schools, community health centers, the YMCA or YWCA, the Boys Clubs and Girls Clubs, the Scouts, and the Big Brother/Big Sister programs are all excellent resources as well.

If you have a special interest, such as providing friendship to medically fragile children or mentoring to teen parents, mention that as you make your calls. Also feel free to speak up about any special skills you may have, such as musical talents or a hobby you could share. There is no point in being shy about anything that could add to a child's sense of welcome.

If you are over age sixty and of limited income, you may wish to explore opportunities through the Foster Grandparent Program of the federal volunteer agency ACTION. The Foster Grandparent Program is active throughout the nation in a variety of local programs serving children and families. Foster grandparents receive at least forty hours of training, plus transportation costs, meals while volunteering, and a small tax-free stipend; in return, they offer caring, nurturance, and friendship to untold numbers of children nationwide. Programs in which foster grandparents serve vary according to local needs, but may include, for example, providing emotional support to teen parents and their children, or to families affected by abuse or neglect. The national program office is listed in the appendix.

You may have to shop around a bit for the setting and

structure that feel right to you. Particularly if you have little experience with children, a program with a volunteer coordinator and a volunteer training program can offer a smoother, more secure start. At a minimum, look for a setting where both volunteer and paid staff are supported and assisted in keeping the child and families safe and secure.

Keep in mind that many agencies serving children are understaffed. Some may jump at the chance for any willing body who can help, yet not be able to provide structure or support. One college student, for example, volunteered to spend a semester as an assistant youth leader at a children's psychiatric hospital. When she arrived, she learned that the youth leader had resigned and she was expected to lead teen group outings single-handedly. No consistent policies were in place regarding misbehavior, and a drinking incident quickly blew up into a major confrontation, with her in the middle. Although she has since participated happily in other youth programs, that first experience was a major disappointment. It is wise, not only for your own sake, but for the sake of the child or children involved, to insist on any agency structure or support you feel is healthy and useful.

If you don't immediately find a local program offering the exact type of child and family mentoring discussed here, don't be discouraged. Try working within whatever children's programs do exist. Then, if you feel the program could be strengthened by drawing from the extended-family model, you can always advocate for any needed changes. Using the national resources described above, you can offer to help expand the program as needed.

Being a child and family mentor, like being a grandparent, an aunt, an uncle, or a godparent, is an important and meaningful commitment to a child. You offer two gifts to the child: the commitment of unconditional caring, and the willingness to respect, affirm, and supplement the child's existing family. Like all gifts of caring, your involvement may bring deep satisfaction and meaning to you as well.

Four

FOSTER PARENTING

You just can't imagine what it means to see a child come into your home fearful and suffering and lacking in self-esteem, and leave stronger and happier and more whole. Foster parents make a lot of sacrifices, but the rewards we get back are tremendous.

—Gordon Evans
National Foster Parent Association

Foster parenting, like adoptive or birth parenting, is an opportunity to provide and enjoy a loving family life, for and with children. Unlike any other form of parenting, however, each child typically stays for a time period ranging from a few months to a few years. These children's families of birth are experiencing significant problems, preventing the children from safely living at home.

The basic goal of foster parenting is to nurture the child during a time of disruption and stress, providing a healthy and warm family-style life. The goal of the child welfare system, of which foster parenting is a vital part, is to help strengthen and heal the child's family of birth so that the child can safely return. If the foster family, the biological family, and the helping professionals all do their part, the result can be significantly changed and improved lives for an entire family—particularly the children.

Foster parenting isn't easy, and it requires a special kind of person. Patience, fullness of spirit, and a high level of energy are essential. A good sense of humor, and a willingness to accept life as it comes, help as well.

Many foster parents feel that fostering is deeply rewarding in a way that few people can imagine. A caring and capable foster parent can open new doors in the life of a child, at the very time when hope and trust might otherwise be destroyed. On a day-to-day level, foster parenting can often be both satisfying and challenging. For anyone who loves children, it can be a constructive, affordable, practical way to enjoy their company in a family setting. Not uncommonly, it results in some lifelong friendships. This is why, despite the considerable challenges, many devoted people have served as foster parents for ten, fifteen, or even twenty years.

Children entering foster care do so during a stressful period in their lives. Some have been abused, physically or sexually, by a parent or other person; some have been homeless or hungry; almost all have been receiving inadequate care. They may react to these difficulties in a variety of ways, such as withdrawal, aggressive behavior, learning problems, bedwetting, or nightmares.

Yet children in foster care may have surprising strengths as well. Some show a reserve of warmth, fun, and happiness in their nature. Some, who have learned to care for siblings and even parents, show a sense of compassion and responsibility far beyond their years. (These children may need help not to learn to behave but to relax and be a child.) Given a safe, structured, and nurturing foster family setting, many children learn to cope with their difficulties, and may begin to flourish and grow.

Given the difficulties facing children who enter foster care, it is easy to assume that their parents must be truly awful people. Yet this is rarely the case. Probably the most common situation is that of a struggling, young, undereducated, overburdened single mother, who loves her children and cares for them the best she can—but who is very human and fallible. Many parents are in pain themselves from their own rocky childhoods and their own limited prospects, and may express that pain through drug and alcohol abuse, through bursts of aggression (often later regretted), and through running away from their responsibilities in a way that unintentionally leaves their children in danger. Many, although not all, are well motivated to address their problems and improve their relationships with their children.

A disproportionate number of children in foster care are from lower-income families and from racial and cultural minorities. In a society in which opportunity is so heavily limited by what you can afford, where you live, where you went to school, and what color your skin is, these are the families most under stress. Also, higher-income families are better able to hide their problems from the public and from the state.

Foster parents come from all races and may be couples or singles, young adults or elders, and men or women. Many also have biological and/or adoptive children whom they are raising or have raised to adulthood, but this is not necessary. Until recently, most were working- and middle-class families, but this appears to be expanding to include both higher- and lower-income families.

Foster parents may or may not be employed, but in most states the family must at least be self-supporting. Like other families, foster families have shifted over the past few decades from being almost entirely couples, consisting of a wage-earning husband and a childraising wife, to including large numbers of two wage-earner couples and employed single parents.

A unifying trait among successful foster parents, perhaps more than any other group, seems to be the degree to which they truly enjoy children. Foster parents aren't saints; they lose patience and make mistakes like anyone else. But talk to them and see; love of children seems central to the lives of many of the best foster parents.

Becoming a Foster Parent

If you decide to become a foster parent, or think you may be interested, your first official step will be to contact the local office of your state department of social services, or a private social service agency that subcontracts from the state department to provide foster care. (We'll call both "the agency.")

The agency may have an informational or orientation session you can attend. This is a good resource for an overview of foster parenting, and will also give you up-to-date information about the department's current needs, services, and requirements for foster parents.

Ask, too, if there is a local foster parents' group whose meeting you could attend. Their meeting may be more focused on individual issues and immediate problems, but it could also give you the inside scoop on what it is really like to foster parent in your area. Be sure to ask if there is a regular newcomers' meeting.

To become a foster parent, you must be approved and licensed according to state standards, much the way a day-care provider is. In most states, this will mean one or more interviews with a social worker, a visit to your home, and a criminal record check. Try not to worry too much about the interviews and the home visit; just relax and be yourself, and it will probably go fine. Social workers deal with many children who need caring foster families, so their goal is to find nice folks like you, not to judge you or to screen you out on a whim.

To help prepare and support you in meeting the special needs of children in foster care, you'll probably be required to attend a training course. Training courses usually may be taken in evening or weekend sessions and are free of charge. Don't be offended at having to take training classes, even if you are already experienced at childraising. Training sessions will focus on important issues such as how to help the child deal with grief and loss, how children respond to and heal from abuse or neglect, and how to help prepare the child for reunification if and when the family situation improves. You'll also learn how to work with the agency, and what services are available to help you meet the children's needs.

The training program will also acquaint you with the types of children who enter foster care, and help you assess your own strengths and limitations in caring for them. Take advantage of this opportunity, because it can keep you from becoming overwhelmed later. If you think that you could comfortably handle a sibling group of two or three children, but not an equal number of unrelated children, each with his or her own social worker, family history, medical provider, and arrival and departure dates, say so. If you think you are better with physically than mentally handicapped children, or vice versa, that's important to recognize, too. As you address these and other issues, feel free to ask plenty of questions and raise any concerns you may have.

Considering these issues up front is important because later, in the press of daily responsibilities and urgent requests, it is all too easy to get overloaded. The sad fact is that many state social services departments (like many of the families they serve) are strained almost to the breaking point by underfunding. It is not uncommon for desperate social workers to beg soft-hearted foster parents to go beyond their own limits—or even, in the worst cases, beyond legal limits regarding the permissible number of children per home. If this happens to you, *don't give in*. You cannot provide the care that children need if you push yourself beyond your own capacity, and you help to perpetuate an inappropriate practice.

What Children Want

Children who have been in foster care are remarkably consistent in their views on what makes a good foster parent. Thirteen-year-old Rakeem, a friendly, lanky youth who was temporarily separated from his mother when he was ten, clearly expresses that his foster parents passed the acid test.

"They treated me just like I was their own kid," he says, with quiet satisfaction. "Tell people who want to become foster parents, that's the most important thing. Treat the kids like they're your own."

Probably the most important ways to "treat the kids like they're your own" are to show them affection, to respect and encourage their individual interests and talents, and to include them in all family activities. Additionally, because children have a keen eye for injustice (real or possibly imagined) foster parents—particularly those also raising biological children—must avoid even the slightest appearance of favoritism. Everything from praise to chores to discipline to trust should be apportioned with an eye to fairness.

Yet equity does not always mean identical treatment, because different children have different needs. The delicate balance of meeting an individual child's needs while conveying a sense of general family values can be challenging.

Talking with experienced foster parents quickly reveals a wide range of personal styles and experiences. What successful foster parents seem to share, however, is that rare combination of giving generously to the children in their care, but also recognizing that they cannot and should not try to do it all alone. The best foster parents love children, but also value deeply the adult friends, family members, and helping professionals who can consistently offer them friendship, support, and reassurance.

Joys and Frustrations

If anyone knows the joys and frustrations of both parenting and foster parenting, Lynn and Roger Capansky do. Friendly and outgoing, Lynn chatters over coffee in a homey South

Boston accent. Roger, quieter, with a kind face, strikes one as a kind of "1950s" Dad—relieved to leave much of the child-raising to Lynn, but happy to be a part of the hubbub, to take the kids to a ballgame, or to light and tend the barbecue. Roger works as a distributor for a major tire company; Lynn works part-time at a local store, but mainly she considers children her life's work. Over the eighteen years Lynn and Roger have been married, they have had two children by birth, and eight total in foster care (although generally no more than two, and never more than three, at once).

"Kids will drive you nuts," says Lynn, laughing, "and, believe me, I'm talking about *all* kids. Sometimes I wonder if we do a better job with foster parenting than we did when our own children were little. Of course, we were younger then."

Married in their mid-twenties, Lynn and Roger had a son, Rob, three years later, and a daughter, Judy, two years after that. Like any family, they had good times and bad, but basically they loved parenting. Lynn liked being home with the kids, and their house became one of those magnet houses that seemed to attract neighborhood children.

"Thank goodness one of us was practical," says Lynn. "I could have been one of those people who kept popping out a new baby every couple of years, and we could all live in the poorhouse together. Roger said, 'Fine, we love kids, but let's be practical. There's plenty of kids out there already.' So I thought about some different ideas. Going into teaching, running a daycare, maybe just one more baby. Then a friend suggested foster parenting, and that really hit home with us."

"I liked the idea that it was something we could do together, as a family," explains Roger. "Although, to tell you the truth, I think we had a pretty idealized image. I mean, don't get me wrong, in all the important ways it was actually an even *better* experience than we'd imagined. You really get to care about these kids, and family has a whole new meaning. Rob and Judy will sometimes gripe like kids will—'That's mine, he can't play with it'—but basically it's like extra brothers and sisters, or at least cousins, for them. And I really think it's made them better people, more understanding of the world around them." He pauses, looking for the right words. "But I'm not sure we realized in the beginning just how complicated it could all be."

One issue, for example, was ages of children. Initially, because Lynn and Roger enjoyed children of all ages, they expressed no age preference. But with time, they found that children who have been physically abused are sometimes too rough on younger children. (Although the Capanskys never experienced it, some children who have been sexually abused may exhibit aggressive sexualized behavior toward a younger child.)

Fortunately, because they had always encouraged all the children to come to them with any concerns, Judy and Rob spoke up and the problem was nipped in the bud. Still, when Rob was punched by a foster brother two years his senior, Lynn and Roger decided that, in the future, they'd specify only children younger than Rob and Judy.

In general, Roger and Lynn explained, "bad" behavior had not been much of a problem, however. Most of the children had problems, but their behavior was more troubling, heartbreaking even, than mean.

Take Gabrielle, the third child they fostered. Gaby arrived a month after her fourth birthday, a thin, pretty, and terribly shy child. Rob and Judy, at the time seven and five, were excited to be getting a "foster little sister." The last children with the family had been two brothers, age three and four, who stayed almost a year and whom the whole family still missed. As for Lynn and Roger, their hearts went out to Gaby, who stood so bravely by the window, searching for her mother but rarely crying.

Gabrielle, explained the caseworker, had been removed from her mother because of neglect. Although mother and child appeared close, the mother was young (just turned twenty) and overwhelmed, and possibly had a drinking problem. She had had several boyfriends over the past few years, and had moved several times to live with one or the other. (She had been on a waiting list for her own apartment with public housing since before Gaby was born, but the average wait was six years.) The last boyfriend had become violent, and the mother had fled with Gaby but could find nowhere to go. The caseworker went to court with the mother to help her get a restraining order against the violent boyfriend, but, because the boyfriend's name was the only one on the apartment lease, the judge wouldn't evict him. The caseworker said she wished that the mother and child could have stayed together, but she couldn't find housing for them that quickly. Now the mother was staying in a shelter for women, and they'd keep looking for family housing while also exploring the drinking question. Gabrielle seemed a well-behaved if somewhat withdrawn child, but quite honestly, said the caseworker, they didn't know a lot about her.

The second or third day after Gaby arrived, Lynn became concerned. Gaby had stopped waiting by the window but found a new way to comfort herself. Refusing to join the others, she would sit in the corner with her hand down the front of her underpants, rocking. The behavior was embarrassing and disturbing. Lynn made a mental note to discuss the problem with Gaby's caseworker, and continued to try to involve the child in family activities.

That night, at dinner, things seemed better. Gaby

seemed to be settling in, and all three children laughed and acted silly. But after dinner, Gaby crawled into Roger's lap and tried to rub his genital area.

As soon as the children were in bed and asleep, Lynn and Roger called the caseworker at home. The caseworker was surprised but calm. Gabrielle's behavior, she explained, suggested that she may have been sexually molested, possibly (from the family history) by a boyfriend of her mother. In the morning, the caseworker would arrange to have the child receive a sexual abuse evaluation, and would also refer her to a child therapist.

In the meantime, the caseworker talked with Lynn and Roger about how they could handle the situation. She suggested that the masturbating behavior (Lynn flinched a bit at the term, but of course she'd known that's what it was) not be criticized or punished, because this was the child's way of finding comfort and control over her own body. It was, however, a private behavior, and Gaby should be helped to understand this.

The caseworker suggested that, whenever Gaby began to masturbate, Lynn should say something like "Gaby, I know that bodies can be nice, but that's a private way of touching. If you want to keep your hand in your pants, you need to go lie in your own bed until you're done." Then, if necessary, Lynn (not Roger) should gently lead Gaby to her bed and leave her there alone.

If Gaby preferred to stop masturbating and stay in the room with the family, that was fine, too. Either way, when she returned to the family group, she should be welcomed happily. If the other children had questions, Lynn or Roger could simply explain that bodies are nice but private. Certain things, such as touching inside your underpants or going to the bathroom, are best done privately.

"It was reassuring to have all that explained," says Lynn. "And when I thought about it, kids do have a lot of curiosity about their bodies. But I was worried about how Gaby would relate to Roger. Plus it just broke our hearts to think about a young kid like that maybe having been abused."

Roger, more self-conscious, shared his thoughts only when asked. "It's upsetting when a child is robbed of her childhood like that. Maybe if I'd known more what to expect, I would have reacted better. I hate to say it, but that first night Gaby crawled in my lap that way, I jumped up and nearly dropped her. But the social worker explained about how to teach her about better limits without scaring her off. If she climbed into my lap, I could give her a hug, then set her on a chair right beside me. The truth is, kids who've been abused don't *want* to have to relate that way, it's just that they think it's the only way they'll be accepted."

The pain Gabrielle carried didn't disappear overnight. In many ways, it will be a part of her always. Yet, with occasional setbacks, Gaby did settle in happily with her foster family, and her sexualized acting out diminished with time.

Swallowing what they knew was unfair anger against Gaby's mother ("I knew it wasn't her fault," says Lynn, "but I kept thinking she should have known somehow and done something to protect Gaby from whoever it was"), Lynn and Roger agreed that, for Gaby's sake, they should make her mother feel welcome to visit often. After some initial distrust on both sides, they developed a sort of big sister and brother relationship, and came to admire the young woman's spunk.

Gaby stayed for eight months, then went back with her mother. About a year later, during another family crisis,

Gaby returned to foster care. This time Gaby's mother requested Lynn and Roger, and Gaby returned to them for two months. Afterward, the families stayed friends. Although Gaby visits to this day, she never again needed foster care.

"Sometimes, I'd get so worried about them," says Lynn. "Because, for a long time, it always seemed there was some new problem. Toni [Gabrielle's mother] would get a job, but then lose it because the school called and Gaby was sick and Toni would miss work. Or she'd finally find an apartment she could afford, but it would turn out to have lead paint. And, over the years, she had two more kids, when it seemed to me it was hard enough with just the one. But, on the whole, they've done pretty well, considering. It's a whole other world out there for a woman raising kids alone.

"Gaby, well, she's had some problems in school, and she's been in therapy since forever, but basically she's a great kid. She's twelve now, and just a nice, nice person. She's sure meant a lot to us, and we've tried to let her know how special she really is."

The Sensitivities of Children with a History of Abuse

Lynn and Roger's experience demonstrates how the general rule to "treat kids like they're your own" must sometimes be adjusted slightly to respect the sensitivities of individual children. As Gabrielle showed them, and the social worker explained, children who have been abused may have very different needs and limits from children who have not. Most young children can safely and comfortably sit in the lap of a healthy, nonabusive adult male. A child who has been sexually abused may not be able to, because it creates a level of physical intimacy that may awaken the child's trauma.

Similarly, some child development specialists believe that occasional spanking of a child who has never been physically abused may not be traumatic—but almost all agree that any form of physical discipline is generally extremely traumatic for a child who has experienced past physical abuse. In most states, foster parents are not permitted to spank, strike, or otherwise use physical discipline with a child in foster care, although physically restraining a child from self-injury or harm to others is permissible.

Many successful foster parents approach this issue by quietly setting standards for the whole family that will avoid harm to any. Spanking, for example, is not necessary to child discipline, and may be at least somewhat traumatic for all children. It's a good idea to keep it out of the parental role altogether, for any children. This protects children who may be especially vulnerable, while also avoiding the plaintive "How come you spank me but never spank Stacey?"

The issue of physical affection may be a little harder to address, because some physical affection is good for children. It is a good idea to say "Okay, nobody gets spankings," but probably not to say "Okay, nobody gets hugs."

Many parents with mixed biological and foster families try to avoid unnecessarily intense levels of physical affection with all children—for example, by not allowing children to sleep in bed with the parents. If limits are set gently (for example, by carrying back to bed a child who wakes up and crawls into the parents' bed), this is certainly not harmful to any child. It may even help children to set limits of privacy that will help keep them safe in the wider world. For the child who may have a history of abuse, this policy helps prevent the reenactment of a trauma and avoids making the child feel like the only one left out.

Yet there are differences between what is appropriate with a child who has been with you since birth, one who has been with you for a year, and one who has just arrived. If there are natural differences you don't want to bring to a lowest common denominator, sensitivity and tact may be needed.

Lynn and Roger, for example, developed a quiet habit they often practiced when Gabrielle and Judy both made a beeline for Roger's lap. Lynn would sit down and take Gaby into her lap, while Judy stayed in Roger's, and together they'd read the girls a story. After the story, both parents would get up and move on to other things. No one felt rejected, everyone enjoyed some family time, and Gaby learned a quiet lesson in appropriate adult-child affection.

Setting careful limits is also important because children in foster care, especially young ones or ones who have experienced severe abuse, may confuse past events with more recent ones. If you sleepily allow your foster son to climb into your bed after a nightmare, he may have another nightmare in your bed about a past incident of sexual abuse—then not be able to distinguish the truth from the dream. If you spank a child in your care for misbehavior, she may confuse the incident with a past beating. Events like these, in addition to being traumatic for the child, could lead to a misleading or misdirected report of abuse.

Keep in mind, too, that a child who comes to you for foster care may, like Gaby, have experienced past abuse that has not yet been discovered. You should therefore treat *every* child with the gentle-but-firm caring and limits that one who has been abused would need.

Gordon Evans, president of the National Foster Parent Association (and a long-term, happy foster parent), recommends that foster parents never use physical discipline with the children in their care, and never insist on or encourage any type of physical affection that appears to make a child in any way uncomfortable. Additionally, because most sexual abuse is perpetrated by men, foster fathers should try to avoid private, behind-closed-doors time with a child in their care. An outing to the park by the foster dad and kids is fine, but a foster father-son overnight in a tent, or a private conversation in the foster daughter's bedroom, is out.

That such limits are necessary is unfortunate, but they are important for everyone's protection. Remember, too, the basic truth you are teaching the child: that there are plenty of other ways to show love and caring than one-on-one physical intimacy.

The Pain of Loss and Separation

Another difficult issue, both for children in foster care and for foster parents, is the pain of separation. Children entering foster care may do so for their own protection, but they are, at least temporarily, losing everyone they have ever loved or been loved by. The loss is tremendous and may initially be overwhelming. They will need a great deal of reassurance, both to understand what is happening and to cope with their grief. Since many children in care face a series of moves, they may also need help gaining a sense of stability in what may seem like a constantly shifting world.

Foster parents also face issues of loss that, although less extreme than those faced by children, are nonetheless real and painful. Every time a child leaves, a foster parent must say goodbye. This is equally true of any children by birth or adoption, who remain with the family while other children leave. Birth- or adoptive children may even be confused by the departures, secretly fearing that children are being "sent away" for being "bad"—and that they may be next.

Open and honest discussion of the changes taking place is essential to avoid misunderstanding and help all family members understand and adjust. It is also important to acknowledge and share feelings, creating a climate of acceptance and trust. Albums, mementos, and other ways of preserving memories can also help to honor relationships and relieve the sense of loss.

There are no easy answers to dealing with these issues, but some strategies are surprisingly effective. They are, perhaps, best understood through the eyes of someone who lives them.

Albums and Memories

Clara Vasquez never planned to foster parent; she planned to retire. Specifically, she planned to retire from a twenty-some-year career as a teacher, to enjoy her retirement years with her husband, and to frequently visit their three adult children—and the several grandchildren they would by then surely have. It was assumed, a virtual certainty. The family had lived (first together and then, as the children went out on their own, as near neighbors) in the same Brooklyn neighborhood where Clara and her husband, Carlos, had settled in 1947, after arriving from their native Puerto Rico.

But life, as the old song goes, brings surprises. In 1979, Clara and Carlos's oldest son enlisted in the army, where he made a career, married another career soldier, and is currently raising two children in Germany. Then, in 1982, Carlos died unexpectedly of a heart attack, leaving Clara a widow. That same year, Clara's daughter moved with her children to California, following a job opportunity too good to resist. That left one son, unmarried and without children, and in no particular hurry to change either status.

By the time Clara qualified for retirement, she had realized that her choices were to enjoy a quiet life focused on her friends and hobbies, or to reopen her life to a new group of children. She hesitated, but not for long. She chose children.

"In one way or another," Clara explains, speaking at a foster parents' support group, "children have always been my life. Raising them, teaching them, now raising them again." She laughs. "I guess that's just me."

Clara knew about foster parenting from her work as a teacher, because a number of her students over the years had been in foster care for part or all of the school year. She also knew, from listening to her students, how much pain a child in foster care can carry and how crucial a role a foster parent can play. For all these reasons, Clara came to foster parenting with a healthy respect for both its importance and its challenges. Even so, she needed help to bring her best to it.

"The year my husband passed away, I was eligible for early retirement," explains Clara, "and I felt this tremendous urge to quit work, get a houseful of children, and start over. Luckily, a friend stopped me. 'You're running away,' she said. 'You were back at school the Monday after the funeral, and now you want an instant new family before you've even grieved your loss. What will you have to give those kids if you don't take care of yourself first?'

"Well, I was angry when she said that, and I started right off to give her a piece of my mind. And then I wasn't angry, but crying, and I couldn't stop. When I finally calmed down, I realized she was right."

Clara finished out the school year, and one more, filling the emotional gaps in her life in little ways. As a young woman she had enjoyed church, as much for social reasons as for religious ones, but she and Carlos had fallen out of the habit once the children were grown. She decided to begin attending again, and to join a women's circle that met Tuesday evenings. Then she and a friend who had recently been divorced began getting together frequently, confiding, comforting, and often having fun. Clara hadn't forgotten foster parenting; in a quiet way, she was getting ready.

One evening, Clara invited a friend over, and together they sorted through Clara's old family pictures, putting them into an album. It was bittersweet but gave Clara a sense of peace. A few days later, Clara made the call to sign up for foster parenting.

"It was funny about that picture album," Clara says now, "because one of the things they told us in the training was about helping kids make albums of their life story. It could be anything—photos, pictures they draw, something their mother or father gave them, something you give them, anything they want to put in it. Or maybe they're old enough that they want to write down their story, or tell it to you and you write it down. It's a comfort to them, because they feel like they have a way to tie it all together, the different homes, the people they love. Everybody they wish they could have always, all together with nobody hurting anyone, they can have in their albums. I know how they feel, and I always put their pictures in my album, too.

"Not every child wants to do an album, or they'll start and stop, and I don't push them. But most of them really love the chance, even if they find themselves crying partway through. If that happens, I figure, that's all right, they need to cry. I just try to be there for them, to comfort them and explain.

"And I never say anything bad about their parents, even if I feel angry with them myself. I don't lie, I don't say, 'I know your mother loves you' or 'I know your father won't hurt you again' if I don't know those things to be true, because the child can smell a lie. But I will say something like 'Sweetie, sometimes parents love children the best they can, and sometimes that's not good enough. If your parents hurt you sometimes, it's probably not because they don't love you. It's certainly not anything wrong with you. It's probably an adult problem that they need help from another adult with.'

"Then, if I know the parent is trying to get help, like therapy or drug treatment, I'll try to explain that to them, in terms they can understand. The child may or may not respond, but at least I know that I've given them the information, and maybe it will be helpful to them later."

If life brings surprises, so do surprises bring life, and Clara has found her "retirement" life as a foster mother a rich and fulfilling one.

"What is it about these children?" she muses. "They're surely not better behaved or more appreciative than my own children were, or the ones I taught in school. But they're facing a terrible loss, and they're rebuilding. And I respect them so much for it. Because I've faced my own losses, and rebuilt my own life, and it wasn't that easy—and I'm an adult, with an education, and I've never been abused. For these children, it's so much harder."

Clara catches herself with an embarrassed smile, as if caught in the midst of excessive sentimentality. "Besides, let's face it," she adds, with a characteristic laugh, "there's nothing like kids to spice up your life!"

Maximizing the Foster Parenting Experience

There is no magic formula for successful foster parenting, but a number of basic guidelines have proven useful for many foster parents. The following points may serve as a helpful starting place:

- Before, during, and after foster parenting, take care to maintain and nurture your own support system. You'll need energy to meet the needs of the children, and a caring support system can help.
- If you have experienced losses, whether the loss of family or of the dream of a certain type of family, take time to nurture yourself before you begin foster parenting.
- Take full advantage of any foster parent training program available to you. A good training program can help tremendously as you meet new challenges.
- Be aware that the social worker and the agency can be an important resource in helping you meet the child's needs. Be prepared to get involved in decision making, and don't be afraid to ask for help.

- Remember that the social worker and the agency who have custody of the child or children in your care have a responsibility to the child, the child's parents, and to you. Be persistent in any requests for needed services, insisting on meeting with supervisors or administrators, and getting answers in writing, if necessary.
- Consider joining or starting a foster parents' group in your area. Such a group can be a wonderful source of help and support, can increase your political clout with the agency placing children, and can help the children in your care to form friendships with other children who share their experiences.
- Never physically discipline a child in foster care. Learn, through training, reading, and practice, about effective, nonphysical child discipline.
- Be affectionate in a friendly way, but avoid levels of physical intimacy that could confuse or produce anxiety in a child in foster care. If you have concerns about this, be sure to address them in foster parent training meetings or discussions with social workers.
- If you have other children in your home, consider requesting younger children. If you don't have other children and think you have a talent with teens, by all means consider asking for an older child. Teens and older children are more verbal and more independent. They can be challenging, but the experience can also be very meaningful. You may find that you're likely to be a continuing resource to them as they grow to adulthood.
- Check on whether your state department of social services has insurance coverage that would include injury to or by a child in your care. Also check on the

coverage that your homeowner policy may provide. If you are not satisfied with the coverage, check with your local foster parents' group or the National Foster Parent Association for suggestions.

- Speak as positively as possible about the child's parents in conversations with the child, and extend a friendly hand to them if you can. This type of respect and friendliness is good for the child in that it reduces the feeling of shame and secrecy. (Check with the social worker about whether there are limitations about contact with the parent, however, if safety may be an issue.)
- Remember that your job is to care for and nurture the child, but to help the child move on. Foster parenting may sometimes lead to lifetime friendships, or even adoption, but it's not fair to the child or to yourself to build expectations.
- Try to allow time between when one child leaves your care and another arrives. You'll need to grieve the loss of the child's company, and to rebuild your own energy and enthusiasm.
- Above all, follow the children's golden rule to "treat the children as if they were your own," while also respecting their individual differences.

Foster parenting is at once very different from and very like other forms of parenting. It is not for everyone, but has been deeply satisfying for many. If you love children, and have the ability to do so with patience and hope and without possessiveness, it may well be the right route for you.

Five

ADOPTION

There is no classic type of couple or person who adopts. Some already have children, some don't. Some are single and others married. But they all see the potential in the child being adopted, and want to grow as a family.

—Gloria Hochman
The National Adoption Center

When a child is adopted, a new family is born. As in marriage or childbirth, new bonds are created in an atmosphere of love and hope. For many, adoption begins a new and rich chapter of family life.

For most people who adopt, an agency is the midwife of the adoption. In most states, both private agencies and public agencies are active in every aspect of the process. Agencies approve potential adopters, work with the child's family of origin, obtain parental consents or the termination of parental rights, match children with prospective adopters, and appear in court to help finalize adoptions.

Although different types of adoption differ in the degree to which they depend on agencies, very few adoptions occur entirely without some form of agency involvement. Even if you choose a route that minimizes agency involvement—for example, by finding a pregnant woman yourself who wishes to have her child adopted—you will still typically need to present to the court that is formalizing the adoption an agency's evaluation of your ability to provide a good home. For most adoptions, the agency's role is even more central, extending to every aspect of the process.

This chapter explores the most common type of adoption: a couple or a single adult applies to an agency, is approved to adopt, learns about the children currently available for adoption through that agency or affiliated agencies, and then adopts one or more of the currently available children. Later chapters explore other, more specific types of adoption, but still generally with the agency playing a central role, and still following most or all of the steps described here. In adoption of a child formerly in foster care with the adopters (Chapter 6) or formerly in kinship care with the adopters (Chapter 9), the agency that placed the child in foster care or kinship care usually also facilitates the adoption. In international adoption (Chapter 7), most adopters work with an agency specializing in the placement of children from other countries. Finally, identified adoptions (Chapter 8) involve a personal agreement between the parent(s) and the adopter(s), but an agency still must approve the adopters and may play a facilitating role. This chapter thus discusses what is still the most common form of adoption and also lays the groundwork for understanding the other types.

In the typical agency-based adoption, the agency obtains temporary legal custody of the child to be adopted, either by consent of the parents or, in cases of abuse or severe neglect, by a court process that terminates the parents' rights. The agency then places the child with a couple or, in some cases, a single adult whom it has selected as the adoptive parent(s). The adoption, which is finalized by court order, transfers the child from the temporary legal custody of the agency to the permanent legal and physical custody of the adoptive parents. Once finalized, the adoption is complete, and the new parents and child have the exact same legal status as any other parents and child.

Types of Agencies and the Children They Place

The two major types of adoption agencies—public agencies and private agencies—differ in their services, their fees, and the type of children they place.

The *public agency* typically is a branch of the state social services department and likely has an office in your county. Children placed by public agencies range from babies to teens, represent all races and cultures, and have a variety of needs. Many are in foster care while awaiting adoption, and may have been in foster care for some time before becoming available for adoption.

Most infants placed by public agencies are African American and are placed, if possible, with African American adopters. (See Chapter 1 for discussion of this policy.) Public agencies usually place very few European American infants.

Many children placed by public agencies have special

emotional and/or physical needs or limitations but are otherwise usually in good health. A good number have been waiting months or even years for adoption, because of difficulties in finding homes for them or because of the system overload that can lead to children slipping through the cracks. Some of these children have siblings, and social workers try to keep them together in the adoption.

Because as many as 35,000 children nationwide are awaiting placement at any one time, people who wish to adopt through a public agency or its subcontractor can often do so without either long waits or significant expense. Adoption fees are generally modest and/or waivable, and even the lawyer's fee (generally $1,000 to $1,500) may be paid by the state.

In fact, federal legislation provides that children classified by a state, county, or district as "special needs" may continue to receive medical coverage and that their adoptive parents may receive monthly stipends for their care if necessary, even after the adoption is complete. In many localities, "special needs" is defined very broadly. In some states, for example, special needs includes any child over age six awaiting adoption, any child who has been in foster care for a significant period of time, any child of a race or culture that is overrepresented among those children needing homes, and/or any sibling group.

Children may also be adopted through purely *private adoption agencies*, which are state-licensed, nonprofit or for-profit organizations. Private agencies usually specialize in the type of child they place. Some place primarily children from Jewish or Catholic birthparents. Others place only infants, often by acting as the intermediary with birthmothers. Some specialize in children with special challenges, such as Down's syndrome. Some specialize in international adoptions, as discussed in Chapter 7.

Some of the common differences between public and private agencies are much like the common differences between public and private schools. Adoptions through a private agency (with some exceptions) tend to be expensive. You pay a fee, commonly $2,000 to $5,000, for the private agency's services; you may also, in the case of infant adoptions, pay as much as $5,000 to $10,000 or more for the medical care and living expenses of the biological mother and child during pregnancy and immediately after the birth. (You may have additional expenses, including, typically, $1,000 to $2,000 for legal services, but this is generally not paid to or through the adoption agency.) In return, you may receive more time and attention, perhaps in more pleasant surroundings, from workers who may be better paid and have lighter caseloads. However, you may find a long waiting list at the private agency, particularly if it specializes in infants or young children without identified special needs.

Some private agencies subcontract from the state agency, placing some children from the state's caseload. Sometimes a subcontracting private agency focuses on a particular type of placement that the state agency has not been successful enough in promoting. A few programs, for example, have focused on placing African American children with like families, with excellent success. Other subcontracting private agencies simply act to relieve a general caseload overload in the state agency.

In general, subcontracting private agencies have a child population similar to that of the state agency, and have all the advantages of subsidized costs, medical coverage, and adoption subsidies that the state agency does. They may or may not have the overcrowded caseloads that many public agencies do.

If you are interested in considering adoption through a private agency subcontracting from the state agency, simply call the adoption placement unit of the state agency and ask if they have any affiliated private agencies working with them. Or you can call local private agencies to ask whether they work with the state agency and to learn about their policies.

Who Can Adopt?

Just as agencies differ in the types of children they place, they may also differ in the types of adopters they seek. A few may adhere to very traditional standards, seeking only married couples of a highly restricted age range, income level, and educational background, but such rigidity is no longer common. Most agencies now recognize that healthy families need not be defined by old stereotypes. Today a wide range of loving adults can and do adopt.

Nonetheless, each agency retains its own basic requirements. Public agencies (and private agencies that subcontract from them) tend to be more flexible in their requirements than purely private agencies. Additionally—and unfortunately—agency selectivity may vary with the degree to which the child being sought is in demand. If you want an infant, you must often meet far more traditional standards than if you want to adopt a waiting child. Singles, for instance, may be encouraged only to adopt an older child or one with special needs—even though a child with special needs may present challenges that may be more difficult for a single parent to meet.

Most agencies do begin with basic eligibility guidelines for prospective adopters. Commonly, they include the following:

Age. You must be at least eighteen, and many agencies require that you be at least twenty-one. Upper age limits vary dramatically by agency, with a few as low as thirty-five, and some (primarily public agencies) with age limits as high as sixty.

Marital Status. Some agencies are concerned about the length of the marriage; others are concerned about its stability. Although the Child Welfare League of America's recommended standards state that single adopters should not be automatically disqualified, some adoption agencies will not work with single adopters.

Health. A medical exam is usually required. Many agencies placing infants require medical evidence of infertility.

Religion. Some private agencies require you to have the same religion as the child or the child's birthparents. Others require that the adopters be able to show some level of religious commitment.

Income. Some private agencies may require that you meet a minimum income level. Most public agencies require only that you be able to show you are self-supporting.

Family Size. When placing an infant, some private agencies require that the adopters be childless or have no more than one child. Public agencies, however, sometimes favor adopters with childraising experience and often do not have strict limits on family size.

The most important qualities of adopters cannot be measured by numbers but are explored throughout the adoption process. These include the capacity to nurture, the willingness to stand by a commitment, and the dedication to—and joy in—family life.

The Long Road to Family

"We're your perfect traditional family," laughs Paula Gaither, talking with her husband, Will, "one girl, one boy, two years apart. It only took us about fifteen years to manage it."

By Will and Paula's count, they spent about three years trying to get pregnant without medical intervention, three more years with medical help, and three years waiting to adopt their oldest child, Shana, whom they adopted as an infant through a local private agency. Four years later, they returned to the same agency, and to other private agencies, and were dismayed to learn that both the wait and the fees for adopting an infant had increased substantially. By the time another infant was available, Shana would be in at least second or third grade—and the adoption's cost would cut heavily into what they considered their savings for their children's education.

After exploring and thinking about their options, Paula and Will decided on a compromise route. When Shana was six, they adopted their second child, Jason, at age four. The adoption was arranged through their local department of social services, involved minimal wait, and cost them less than $2,000. To a visitor today, at least, seeing the family together, with the children alternately climbing into parental laps, asking to be read "just one more" story, or playing together in the yard, it all seems to have worked out very well indeed.

"The kids are great," says Will. "That's the best part. The work and the responsibility, that's the worst part. As for the way we did it, well, there are pros and cons for each route."

"I've always loved babies," says Paula, "and it was great to have Shana almost from her birth. Even so, as she got older, as a toddler and a preschooler and then school age, she got more and more exciting. I guess I became less wedded to the idea that you have to start with an infant. Don't get me wrong—adopting Shana as an infant was a wonderful thing, and I'm so grateful we could do it. But we couldn't do it again, and adopting Jason has been equally wonderful."

Health issues were a major concern for Paula and Will. "To tell you the truth," says Paula, "we wanted our kids to be basically healthy, physically and mentally. If they turn out to have serious problems, we'll love them just the same, but I really, really hope they won't."

Because health was a priority for them, Paula and Will found out all they could prior to adoption about the children's medical and family history, including any known health conditions or risks. (This is important even if you are open to a child with known health problems, because you'll be better equipped with more knowledge, as will their health care providers.) They soon learned, however, that there were no guarantees, either with newborns or with older children.

Once they stopped looking for guaranteed perfection, however, Will and Paula found it possible to identify and adopt children who were likely to be basically healthy. Shana is friendly and outgoing, with a lively sense of humor. She also has some learning disabilities, and requires special tutoring in reading and writing. Jason is an affectionate son and a good student. He also is in therapy to address his issues of loss and help him control his occasional bursts of overwhelming anger. Will and Paula have learned, like many of the best adoptive parents, to see their children as themselves, and to celebrate their progress and growth on their own terms, not by comparison with real or imagined norms.

"Our other big concern was bonding," says Will, "and how to talk with the kids about being adopted. We've had to learn a lot, but fortunately there are lots of resources available. These days, so many kids are adopted, or have stepparents, or whatever. There are books for kids about being adopted, and for parents on how to talk with them. Many teachers understand, and can help smooth the way with other kids. Also, we belong to an adoptive family group, so many of our friends and our children's friends are from adoptive families."

Again, the issues were slightly different for Shana and Jason. Will and Paula never had any direct contact with Shana's birthparents, and neither they nor the birthparents learned each other's last names. They were provided with a basic family and medical history, however, and a short, caring note from Shana's birthmother, which Paula and Will put in her baby album. Beginning when Shana was about two years old, and still to this day, looking at the album together has been a favorite shared activity.

At the first page, Will or Paula point to the note and say, "This is a note to you from your birthmother, the woman whose body you grew inside before you were born," and then read the note aloud. Then they turn the page to a picture of them with Shana when she first came to them, and say, "And here you are with us, the very first day we adopted you. That was such a happy day!" In addition to being at the center of a much-loved ritual, the album provides a natural way to begin conversations about how they became a family.

Jason also has an album, which reflects his own unique

history. He came to them remembering both his biological mother and the foster family where he had recently been living, and was actively grieving the loss of people he had loved and depended on. He needed immediate help with understanding not simply what had happened but why. Above all, he needed help dealing with his feelings of grief, loss, and fear of abandonment. His continuing therapy, in which Paula and Will have participated, is one way he is supported in this. The making of his album, which he participated in from the beginning, has been intertwined with his therapy. It includes his own drawings and autobiography, as well as pictures of his family of origin and other mementos that were saved from his early years.

To help Jason feel less cut off from his past, Paula and Will became friendly with his former foster family so that Jason could continue to feel they were nearby and available. They also accept, through the agency, any letters from Jason's birthmother and work with Jason's therapist as to whether, when, and how to share them with Jason.

Will and Paula have talked a great deal about whether they would permit visits by either child's parent, if a parent so requested through the agency. So far they think not, and to their knowledge neither child's parents have requested any visits. They do feel strongly, however, that if either child, as an adult, wants to find his or her birthparents, they will assist in every way possible. To help keep this possibility open, each of the agencies involved, at their request, obtained appropriate written consents from each birthmother, stating that the agency could release identifying information if so requested by the child after age eighteen.

Perhaps the main way that Paula and Will address their children's concerns, however, is simply to offer them love, caring, honesty, and constancy. It seems to work; the children are lively and affectionate and, despite occasional storms, seem basically happy.

"We're lucky, lucky folks," says Will, ruffling Jason's hair as the child climbs into his lap. "I count my blessings all the time."

The Adoption Process

Typically, the adoption process includes gathering information and contacting agencies, the application process, the home study and preparation, the matching with a child, the preadoptive placement, and the legal process. Each new step brings you closer to your goal, and can be an important opportunity for growth and learning.

For both information and support throughout the entire adoption process, you may want to join and become active within a local organization of adoptive parents or a local chapter of a national organization listed in the appendix. More experienced adopters can offer you a sympathetic ear, and many groups actively advocate on behalf of adoptive families both locally and on the national level. Through their workshops, newsletters, books, and informal exchanges, adoption support groups can be excellent information sources.

Through a group, you can learn which local agency might best fit your needs and whether things are going as they should during the adoption process. If not, you may receive helpful ideas on how to correct the situation. After the adoption, these groups provide a supportive environment where you can air your concerns and get advice on parenting an adopted child—as well as enjoying the friendship of families who share a special bond with your own. A listing of national and regional groups is available in the appendix.

Gathering Information

With so many specialized adoption agencies, and so many different types of children to adopt, you may feel a bit overwhelmed. A good first step is to gather information. An excellent resource, available in bookstores and libraries, is *The Adoption Resource Guide*, written by Julia Posner and published by the Child Welfare League of America. A more immediately available resource is the list of local agencies in your phone book's Yellow Pages, although it will not give you the range of information on services, fees, and policies you'll find in a published resource guide.

Contacting Agencies

When you call an agency, you'll first want to be sure you have reached the person who can give you the information you need. This is especially important if you are calling your state social services department, which is probably a large organization with many different units. So start with a friendly "Hello, I'm interested in information about adopting a child through your agency. May I speak to a worker in your adoption unit who could help me?"

When you are transferred, repeat the statement, until you connect with someone who says "Yes, I can help you." At that point, introduce yourself by name, and write down the name of the person who is assisting you, so you'll be able to call again with any other questions.

During this first discussion, you need not describe your circumstances in full or learn everything about adoption or about the agency. Rather, you'll want to focus on basic information that can help you determine if this agency can assist you in reaching your adoption goals. Suitable questions might include the following:

- Are you currently accepting applications for adoption? If not, are you taking names for a waiting list?
- Could you give me some general information about the children for whom you are currently seeking adoptive homes, such as most common ages, needs, and so on?
- What are your requirements for adoptive parents? Are there exclusions based on [add what you think is of concern, such as income level, religious affiliation, or marital status]?
- What fees are involved? May they be paid in installments? Can fees be waived, or is there a sliding scale?
- What is your home study process? Will I participate in completing the home study document? Will I receive a copy?
- Do you offer an adoptive parent training program? Postadoption support and assistance? Could you describe your services?
- Could you send me some written information about adopting through your agency?

The Application

The agency's application form, which will be mailed to you or provided when you visit, will contain questions on basic information such as your income, your type of work, your race, your religion, and the length of your marriage. It may also ask for a short explanation of why you want to adopt.

Often, potential applicants are invited to attend an agency's next regularly scheduled open house, where a group of prospective adopters will learn how the agency operates and what sort of children it has available. A catalog of the agency's waiting children may be available, as might a catalog maintained by the region's adoption exchange. At the end of the open house, those who wish to apply are given applications.

The next step, the intake interview, will sometimes take place immediately after the application forms are turned in. More often, it will occur after one or more social workers have reviewed your form. If applying with a spouse, you may be interviewed together and then separately. You will be asked to discuss your marital history, childhood, reasons for adopting, even your physical and mental health. Some questions may be sensitive: Is there a divorce or spotty work history in your background? Have you had psychiatric problems? Have you ever been convicted of a crime? These and other questions may arise as the social worker tries to get a sense of your strengths and possible difficulties as a potential parent.

If an issue in your background could cause the social worker concern—you once declared bankruptcy, for instance, or have been previously divorced—you must be prepared to address the issue in a positive light. A bankruptcy or a divorce could mean, for instance, that you have learned from the hard times and have become a stronger person as a result. For a child who has seen his or her share of trials, such a parent could be a good model.

Perhaps you have applied to an agency that has a religious affiliation. While you may have the same affiliation (it isn't always necessary, by the way), you may be asked whether you attend services. Either way, be prepared to discuss your views. You might note—if it is true—the aspects of your values or your spirituality that you believe will benefit a child.

Above all, be honest and try not to be defensive during the interview. You may be tempted to be less than frank, but dishonesty is almost sure to backfire. Many things, such as a past divorce, a criminal conviction, or serious family problems, are certain to be discovered during the evaluation process anyway. More important, though, honesty is necessary out of fairness to the child. If a policy is discriminatory, by all means contest it, or choose a different agency. But pulling a child into a web of deceit is wrong and possibly dangerous.

The interview should last about an hour or two, and at its end you should be able to learn your chances of acceptance by the agency. Don't expect a firm answer, however, since the agency may use a committee to review applications.

If you are accepted, the social worker who conducted the interview will often be assigned to work with you for the duration of the adoption. If you are not accepted, you should be told why and whether you can appeal that decision to anyone. Remember, too, that other agencies exist. The more flexible you can be in your adoption goals, the more likely you are to be approved.

The Home Study and Preparation

After the application process, the next step is the home study and preparation. In part the home study is intended to help the agency's worker understand more about your home and family, and thus facilitate a match with a child whose needs fit your abilities. It also helps you learn about adoption and the child to be adopted, and prepares you for this important step in family growth. The home study results in a home study document, which is used by the agency, and perhaps other agencies and adoption exchanges, in matching with a child for adoption.

Your first task in the home study is to provide the agency with some paperwork. The agency will need birth certificates for you and your spouse, a marriage certificate, record of divorce (if any), and death certificate of any deceased spouse. These must be certified copies—that is, copies produced by the official bureau that handles those records, not photocopies. Marriage, divorce, death, and birth certificates are typically provided by the county where they were issued. Some records, such as death certificates, are available from the Office of Vital Statistics or Vital Records, a part of state government, in the state where the event occurred.

Along with these documents, you will need to provide proof of employment, financial records, and a statement from your doctor regarding your physical, and sometimes your mental, health. Other documents you may need to provide include a physician's statement certifying infertility (usually only in the case of adoption of infants), certified copies of the birth certificates of any children now in your family, and an autobiography of yourself and your spouse.

You will also have to provide a list of references, people who may be called on to write letters of recommendation about you or may be interviewed by the agency's social worker by phone or in person. These references should have agreed in advance to do this and be able to tell you pretty much what they will say. If a letter of reference is required, you could ask to see it before it is mailed.

Most important, your references should be chosen with an eye to whether they can evaluate your abilities as potential parents. Friends who are already parenting are a good choice, as are community or religious leaders. If you volunteer or work with children, someone on the staff of that organization would be an excellent choice. If you are already a parent, you have a host of people to choose from, such as your child's teacher or your next-door neighbor. The references you supply should be people who feel close to you and can speak well of your decision to adopt and your ability to parent.

The Changing Home Study

In a traditional home study, the agency social worker will visit you at home for an in-depth interview and a chance to look at the house itself and the room the child will occupy. The visits may take place over several weeks, but will typically be done by the same social worker first assigned to your case. The visiting social worker will address the more sensitive issues raised in your intake interview and will explore how you relate to each other, to children, and to your community at large. Many social workers, and many agencies, see this process as having a strong education and support aspect—not just to spot potential problems but to help address and resolve them early.

How some agencies conduct the home study has undergone some recent changes. Now some agencies, primarily those serving older children and children with special needs, take an informal approach, using a group process that is as much a parental training session as an evaluation. Meeting over a several-week period, the group might spend one night writing their autobiographies, another discussing how they believe adopted children feel about the process. They might spend the final night meeting with a family that has adopted. "Many times," observes Eileen Ginty of the Massachusetts Adoption Resource Exchange, "adopters meet and form their own support networks through these groups."

Overall, the objective of a group home study is to educate you and help you evaluate the concept of adoption, not to put you under a microscope. If you are considering adopting a special needs child, you'll need information and support. The group process can help *you* decide whether you are able to meet the child's needs.

Who writes the home study document has also become more flexible. In traditional home studies, it is written by the caseworker and cannot be altered by the adopters. Today some agencies permit prospective adopters, working with the social worker, to write their own home study document. Many more permit adopters to insert autobiographies and/or pictures into the document. Adopters may also have an opportunity to review the completed home study document to verify its accuracy.

Because the home study document represents you in the adoption process, it is vital that you take an active role in completing it. If you can insert autobiographies or statements on why you want to adopt, do so. If you can include photographs, include several copies of those that show you in your home and in family settings. If the packet will be sent to a foreign agency, be sure that it contains nothing that might offend that nation's culture and that it emphasizes whatever cultural and ethnic diversity already exists in your life.

Most people feel the home study process leaves them vulnerable. Uncomfortable as it may be, try to remember that it is for the child's protection and welfare. If you feel highly defensive and invaded, think over the process carefully, perhaps discussing it with a trusted friend or counselor. Possibly your discomfort comes in part from your own internal concerns.

If, for example, you feel very unresolved and anxious about some aspects of your relationship with your own parents, it would be natural to strongly dislike even well-meaning questions on the topic. Yet parenting does raise issues about how we were parented, and such questions may be helpful and appropriate as you explore adoption. The same may be true of other sensitive areas, such as your relationship with your spouse, how you handle anger and conflict, and so on.

This does not mean, however, that you must be submissive or hide your feelings. You have rights in this process, including the right to be treated fairly and with respect. If you don't understand why certain questions are relevant, you can ask why they are being asked. If you feel a particular social worker persistently views you negatively or is excessively intrusive, you can express your concerns. Start by talking directly with that person, politely and calmly stating what you'd like to see done differently, rather than blaming or sounding critical. If that doesn't work, you could initiate a similar discussion with the social worker's supervisor. It is perfectly acceptable to request a different social worker or to switch to a different agency, if you think that move will provide you with a more positive, nurturing support system.

The home study report, when completed, is the only means by which other workers and other agencies can evaluate your true willingness and ability to adopt and nurture the child you are seeking. It should be complete, honest, and fair, and should help you put your best foot forward.

Disseminating Your Home Study Report

When your home study is completed, there may be a child immediately available whom everyone agrees is a good match. Quite likely, however, finding the child you'll adopt will take considerably more work. You can increase your options and reduce waiting time by having your home study sent to other agencies as well, eliminating the necessity of repeating the home study process. This makes a lot of sense, especially if a long waiting list exists for the type of child you hope to adopt.

Because the home study document is your emissary, you should take an active role in its dissemination as well as its development. Be sure to request that your social worker send the entire packet to all agencies you have specified and help you identify others you might have overlooked. (Offer to pay the cost of copying and postage, if this helps.)

With the home study completed and in circulation, the wait begins, the length of which typically depends on both personal and demographic factors. For example, all other things being equal, couples may be able to adopt more quickly than singles, because most adoption workers feel most children benefit from two-parent homes. If the agency is seeking homes for a large number of African American children (as many public agencies are), African Americans may be able to adopt more quickly than European Americans. On the other hand, higher- or moderate-income people may be favored by some agencies—probably unfairly, but it can be a factor. Other factors, such as the efficiency of the agency and the adoption worker, and the rapport developed between the adopters and the worker, may also play a role.

Demographic differences in the children being sought also greatly affect waiting periods. At one end of the scale, many children have been in foster care for years, and the matching and placement process can begin within weeks of their agency receiving a home study document. At the other end, the wait for a white infant without identified physical or mental disabilities can run to several years.

If you are concerned about the likely waiting period, you should talk carefully with your adoption worker about the issue. You may be able to reduce or eliminate the wait by being more flexible in your adoption goals. Be careful, however—don't let impatience tempt you beyond your own realistic limits. Any child you adopt should be one you have the skills and commitment to parent well.

Matching with a Waiting Child

In many adoptions, particularly those involving children older than infants, matching of parental skills and children's needs is an important process, involving exchanging information and making informed decisions. You'll receive information about children immediately available for adoption through notebooks, newsletters, and possibly even videotapes. The adoption workers placing the children will receive information about you through the dissemination of your home study.

Organizations known as adoption exchanges are a primary source of information regarding immediately available children. These nonprofit national and regional organizations publish catalogs containing the pictures and histories of children immediately available for adoption in the geographic region or specialization they serve. The catalogs, called photo-listings, are made available to prospective adopters and social workers at adoption agencies and libraries around the exchange's region. In an effort to place waiting children, for example, a photo-listing book was also recently launched by the State of New York, where the roster of waiting children has jumped from about 750 to over 1,000 since 1987. New York, like most states, does not require that you be a resident of the state to adopt most of the children available.

A similar service is offered by the National Adoption Center (NAC), a Philadelphia-based organization that, in its efforts to promote adoption of special needs children, maintains an electronic network linking public adoption agencies nationwide. This allows more detailed matches such as, for example, a couple in Virginia seeking to adopt a brother and sister between ages three and six with no more than moderate special needs, and two siblings from Arkansas who meet that description.

The children served by the NAC and adoption exchanges typically range in age from early childhood to their teens. Many have emotional or physical difficulties, and many are in sibling groups, with a need to at least maintain contact with the siblings. Because the adoption exchange serves a region, some of the children in its catalog may live outside of your state.

The Massachusetts Adoption Resource Exchange

(MARE), for example, focuses on Massachusetts and Rhode Island children over age eight who often have physical or emotional disabilities. MARE publishes a catalog filled with pictures and profiles of children awaiting adoption throughout the New England region. The catalog contains pictures of each child, along with a physical and psychological profile and a statement of their legal status regarding adoption. Like most other exchanges, MARE also publicizes the children in its catalog through announcements in local newspapers and on television.

The catalogs of one or more adoption exchanges will likely be shown to you when you visit an adoption agency. They are a fine way to get a sense of a child you may want to adopt, and you can express your interest through the adoption agency that referred you.

When you find a child you are interested in adopting, your home study report comes into play. Like other exchanges, MARE does not place children but simply promotes them and, working with home studies, often matches children with adopters referred by local agencies. It may examine several home studies, however, before making a match, says Eileen Ginty, MARE's director of programming. "More people are adopting older children," she notes, "so we're able to look for a good match."

If you send the packet because you are interested in a specific child, include a cover letter expressing your interest and why you think you'd have a lot to offer that particular child. Then follow up to see if you can meet with that child's social worker once he or she receives the packet.

If your request to adopt a specific child is declined, you can ask the agency for an explanation of its decision. Try, as objectively as possible, to listen and understand any concerns raised. The placement worker's highest duty—like yours—must be to the child. If another home would better serve the child's needs, it is right that that home be sought.

If, however, you think that relevant information was overlooked, you can ask to have your file updated to include more accurate information and to have the adoption request reconsidered in light of the full information. You can also ask to meet with the placement worker to discuss the decision and explain your viewpoint. If you have reason to believe that the decision was discriminatory, and not in the child's best interest, you could ask to appeal the decision or at least talk with a supervisor.

The matching process is a time of anticipation and anxiety. Although rarely easy, it can be a deeply moving experience. Try to use this time to grow personally and to increase your readiness to parent. Keep up your other interests and activities, and don't be afraid to turn to others for encouragement and support. Then, when you do find the child or children who will join your family, you'll be ready to move with joy and enthusiasm to the next step.

The Preadoptive Placement

In most states, the child comes to live with the prospective adopters before the adoption is legally completed, in what is generally called a preadoptive placement. This important "getting to know you" time is often filled with great excitement, anticipation, nervousness, and stress. Don't be alarmed if what you had dreamed of as a perfectly happy time doesn't go smoothly. At the same time, don't be afraid to recognize, address, and seek help with any problems that arise. Your adoption worker, other adoptive parents you may know through an adoption support group, and trusted family and friends can be excellent resources during this time.

Infants. If you are adopting an infant, your first days together will be filled with many of the joys and challenges that all new parents with babies face: cuddling, crying, feeding, changing, and, for you, not a whole lot of sleep. Some adoptive parents (like some biological parents, only perhaps more so) find themselves startled by the suddenness of the change in their lives.

Keep in mind that it is completely natural to feel some anxiety. Parenting a small, utterly dependent being is a new and challenging task—particularly if the child arrives on the scene with comparatively short notice. Some frustration and even anger about the child's constant needs is also quite natural.

Many new parents secretly fear that other new parents don't share these mixed feelings, and wonder if they're somehow different and deficient. New adoptive parents may fear that the imagined "difference" or "deficiency" is due to the lack of a biological connection, or of sharing the birth experience.

There are several ways to emphasize the happiness in welcoming your new child while also addressing any anxieties and stresses that arise. First, plan in advance to have trusted friends and family share in both the excitement and the work. Don't think, for example, that it is silly to ask your mother to come stay for a week or two when the baby comes, even though neither you nor your partner is weak and exhausted from labor and childbirth. If you'd find her being there a comfort and a help, by all means ask her.

The same rule of family nurturance should apply to your

dealings with your community and work world, too. If your office offers maternity leave only as childbirth-related medical leave, or doesn't offer paternity leave at all, work in advance to change or adapt these policies. Our country has yet to adopt family-sensitive work policies, and you can and should be prepared to advocate for your own special type of family.

Preschool-age Children. If you are adopting a toddler or preschool-age child, additional considerations may come into play. Although a child beyond infancy may not require the near-constant feeding and changing that many infants seem to, he or she will be dealing with the considerable stress and anxiety of separation from former caregivers. This stress may express itself through crying, anger, withdrawal, or behavioral difficulties. Because the child may not fully use or understand speech yet, direct reassurance may be difficult to give.

The preadoptive period with a younger child may involve learning to comfort and provide a sense of security, while also getting to know and nurture the child's strengths. A sense of structure in the household, with plenty of attention to the child, is helpful. If the child has mementos from his or her earlier life, such as a favorite blanket or toy, allow the child to hold onto them—constantly, if necessary.

It is also important to explain to the child the basics of what is happening and why, in simple terms. Even if the child's language skills aren't fully developed, you can begin the explanations now, and repeat them as the child grows. You should explain, for example, that the birthparents were unable to care for a child. Add that now you will be the child's parent, and that you will be a family together always.

Again, draw on the resources available to you, including adoption worker, support group, friends, and family, and allow yourself ample time off from work.

School-age Children. The younger school-age child will also be struggling with issues of separation and loss, but with significant differences. First, the child will likely be verbal and able to discuss, at least in simplified terms, the changes occurring. Second, school-age children are in the process of developing their own sense of autonomy and control in their relationships and in the world around them.

Although children younger than age twelve (or, in some states, thirteen or fourteen) are generally not legally permitted to consent or to refuse consent to be adopted, the emotional reality is that they can and should have a voice in deciding their own future. For this reason, the preadoptive placement of school-age children should truly be a mutual "getting to know you" process. Be prepared for lots of questions, as well as some "testing" behavior that asks, in effect, "If I misbehave, will you hurt me or send me away?" Structure and setting of limits are appropriate, but keep in mind that this is a time of building mutual trust, and excessively rigid demands and discipline could undermine that spirit.

Allowing the child's own identified needs and desires to count in the decision-making process also affirms the child's sense of autonomy. Telling the child "You've come to live with us because we're going to adopt you" could make the child feel frightened, undermined, even trapped. A far better approach would be to explain: "We wanted you to come live with us because we'd like to become a family. We hope that we can become your parents, and that you'll want to become our daughter [or son] forever. That process is called adoption, and we can go to a judge, like when people get married, to make that happen."

Teens. With a teenager, the preadoptive period will similarly be a time of building, testing, and negotiating a relationship, but at a more advanced level. Many teens will have significant ties with their families of origin or others from their past, and these should be respected. Generally, unless the teen would be endangered by contact with the family of birth, any contact the teen wants should be permitted and facilitated.

Open adoption (involving some continued contact with the birthfamily) or permanent guardianship (the acceptance of parental responsibility throughout the child's minority, but without terminating the birthparents' rights) may be the preferred route for establishing a permanent family with a teen. These possibilities can and should be explored during the preadoptive period. Talk first with the adoption worker and with a lawyer to be sure you understand the options. Then you may wish to discuss the options and choices with the teen.

Because teens are teens, their "testing" behaviors may be more volatile than the tantrums or misbehaviors of a younger child. You'll want to work closely with the adoption worker, and with any therapist or other care provider the teen may have, and plan in advance to have your own support network firmly in place.

The Final Decision

With a child of any age, the preadoptive period gives you a chance to assess realistically whether you can truly meet that particular child's basic needs and become a workable, nurturing family. That self-assessment begins well before the preadoptive placement, of course, and you would not accept the placement if you felt that the child's needs were beyond your capacity. Yet sometimes, despite the best intentions, prospective adopters enter the preadoptive period with the full intent to adopt, and faith that the plan is a good one—but realize during the course of the preadoptive period that, even with appropriate supports and services, they will not be able to meet the child's needs adequately.

If you feel, during the preadoptive period, that problems are developing, work first, using all available supports, to try to address them. Remember, too, that children don't need perfection from their parents—nor, for that matter, do they offer it. Yet the final decision to adopt is the most serious commitment you will ever make, and it is right and appropriate to make it carefully. If you do have concerns over whether you can meet the child's needs, and do so with the love and enthusiasm that every child deserves, you should discuss your concerns carefully with the adoption worker or others you trust. Ultimately, you must follow your own heart and your own judgment. The decision not to adopt after a preadoptive placement is never an easy one, but in some cases it may be the responsible one.

At its best, the preadoptive period is a time of building, planning, and growing as a family. Although rarely smooth or easy, it is, in many families, remembered with special tenderness as a season of discovery and growing love.

The Legal Process

Close on the heels of the preadoptive placement, and partially overlapping with it, is the legal process of adoption. Since, by law, a child can have only two parents, the first step will be verifying that the parent-child relationship with the family of origin is legally ended. In general, this step occurs before or during the preadoptive placement. If the rights of the biological parents have not already been terminated, the birthmother must sign a form consenting to the adoption.

Birthfather rights are generally identical to birthmother rights if the parents were married at the time of conception or birth, or if paternity was established. If either situation is true, consent from the birthfather will also be needed. If there was no marriage or establishment of paternity, the birthfather's rights, and the requirements regarding them before adopting, vary by state.

If parental rights were terminated previously, a representative of the placing agency, as guardian, will sign the consent to adoption form. The parent or guardian must also sign a consent form permitting you to seek medical treatment for the child if needed before the adoption is legally complete.

Another crucial legal document is the adoption agreement. Signed by you as adopter and by the agency, this agreement is a key tool for safeguarding your child's future and may well be the most important document you will ever sign. The adoption agreement sets out your rights and responsibilities in the adoption process, your child's rights during and after the adoption, and the agency's responsibilities.

The adoption agreement, although always important, is most crucial in the adoption of a child who has, or may have, special medical and therapeutic needs. Under rules established by the federal Child Welfare and Adoption Act, medical coverage of the child under Medicaid may be continued through the state social services department.

To safeguard your child's right to this coverage, it should be specified in the adoption agreement. (Even if you have a family health insurance policy, a health or emotional condition that seems manageable now could escalate into a financial nightmare—and a private insurer could refuse to cover it as a "preexisting condition.") Additionally, if general finances are a problem, the adoption agreement could guarantee a continuing adoption subsidy payment, up to the amount of a regular foster care payment.

Unless these points and any other needed services are specified in the adoption agreement, they will not be guaranteed. For this reason, it is essential that you consult with a lawyer—your own lawyer, not the agency's—who specializes in child welfare issues to get assistance in negotiating and reviewing the adoption agreement. Then work with the lawyer as well as the caseworker; read everything, discuss any concerns or ideas, and ask any questions you may have. This is an important document that will protect your future family, and there is no point in hiring an extra mind and then turning off your own.

The final legal formality will be a court hearing, which generally takes place after the child has been with you for some time in preadoptive placement. The amount of time before the final hearing will vary depending on state legal requirements, the age of the child, and the particular family circumstances. In some cases, more than one hearing may be required.

At the final hearing, the judge will review the home study and information on the child's needs, and decide whether the adoption is in the child's best interest. As ominous as this sounds, it generally goes without a hitch, because everyone involved—the agency, the adopters, the birthparents, and, if old enough, the child—have already agreed. In fact, barring any unusual problems, the final hearing will probably last only a few minutes.

The judge will also rule on whether the expenses you have incurred in the adoption were prudent and fair. You should be aware, however, that since adoption hearings often take place long after the placement of a child, few judges will raise objections to anything in the expense report. As one judge told *California Lawyer* magazine: "It's a happy time at that point. You're not about to start asking questions and looking into shenanigans."

Therefore, if you have concerns as to whether the charges made for the agency's or attorney's services are fair, you should raise them yourself at this point. Even more important, if you have concerns about the adoption agreement, or whether the agency is adequately providing services your child is entitled to receive, these, too, should be raised. Some judges have ordered agencies to return money to adopters, or have amended the adoption agreement to include additional benefits for the child, says Mary Beth Seader of the National Committee for Adoption.

At the conclusion of the hearing, the judge will issue an order that makes the adoption final. Then you can celebrate: legally as well as emotionally, you are a family!

Postadoption Joys and Challenges

In 1983, after unsuccessful attempts at conceiving, Herb and Terri Smith were advised by doctors that they were infertile as a couple. Initially, they thought they'd adopt an infant.

They found, however, that there was a three-year wait, and, in their New Jersey region, they were quoted cost estimates of up to $35,000. (This figure is unreasonably high, according to the National Committee for Adoption, which publishes a list of the average costs for various aspects of an adoption.) The news was, to say the least, discouraging, since they didn't want to wait and didn't have the needed money. Determined not to be deterred, however, Terri suggested they consider a waiting child, possibly with disabilities.

"I'll be honest," says Herb now. "I was not initially enthusiastic. I really had to struggle with my own prejudices, and decide how important parenting was to me. It wasn't an easy decision, and it hasn't been an easy life."

Eventually, Herb and Terri adopted Cindy, an eight-year-old child with a sunny nature and severe physical disabilities. A few years later, they adopted Ricky, also at age eight, and also wheelchair-bound. Both times, there was no wait and no cost. Both children still have—and need—medical coverage and monthly adoption subsidies.

Yet, as the agency had advised them to expect, difficulties lay ahead. People they met on the street would sometimes pull back their own child from the Smiths' new son "like he's got something contagious." Their daughter, although perfectly lucid, would see people addressing questions about her to her parents.

The children themselves also presented challenges. Ricky suffered from severe depression and anger, bearing scars from a long history of abuse and neglect, and was not able to relate well to others as he grew. Now a young man, Rick will soon enter a halfway house for handicapped adults, where his parents hope that he will find companionship and some self-sufficiency. Says Herb, "There's a limit to our abilities, our patience, and how much we can do for him."

Cindy, on the other hand, showed remarkable resilience. She had been raised as a young child by a loving single mother until the mother died. Then, although spending the next few years in institutional care, she had drawn warmth from the staff there and had learned basic life skills. Although Cindy's physical limitations are by far the greater of the two children's, with physical movement limited to the ability to talk and move a pointer-stick with her teeth, Cindy has gained the greater ability to interact with the world around her.

Today, Cindy Smith has graduated from high school and is considering college. To her parents, she is a successful young woman, of whom they will be forever proud.

The Smiths say they are no saints. "Most people have in them the ability to raise troubled kids," observes Herb. "It just takes persistence and extraordinary patience." And the couple received much help from state social services departments and vocational rehabilitation departments, although the help was never volunteered but always sought out. In fact, the Smiths relocated after some years to Michigan, primarily because it offered some of the best free services available nationally for severely handicapped children.

Incidentally, Herb and Terri chose to adopt because they believed they could not have a biological child. Five years after they adopted, Terri gave birth to a daughter; two years later, another daughter was born.

"I guess," laughs Herb, "Cindy and Rick got us into the parenting mood."

Six

ADOPTION BY A FOSTER PARENT

When a child has close emotional ties with a foster family, and becomes ready and available for adoption, then adoption by the foster family can be a wonderfully healthy and happy choice. The newly adoptive parents already know, care about, and are committed to that particular child. For the child, it means more stability, less disruption, and a gentle transition into a permanent new family.

—Linda Kurtz
New York Department of Social Services

If your goal is to adopt a child, foster parenting should *not* be viewed as a route to adoption. If, however, your goal is to provide a loving home and to share a sense of family with a child, for as short or long a period as the child might need—or if you are already foster parenting a child who has now become available for adoption—a fostering-to-adoption route may be just right for your family. Many children are adopted by their former foster parents, an arrangement that may provide a uniquely happy result for all concerned.

If this distinction seems complex and potentially confusing to you, you are absolutely right. The distinction between willingness to adopt and seeking to adopt is subtle, but it is worth exploring and understanding. As we have already seen, one responsibility of a good foster parent is to help the child prepare to return to the family of birth when the parent(s) have resolved the problems that led to the family breakup. That may mean, for example, helping to arrange parent-child visits, helping the child understand the parent's problems, and perhaps remaining as a resource even after the child returns home. Imagine, then, how unfair it would be to take on those tasks while secretly hoping to adopt the child. In effect, fostering while hoping to adopt would be hoping that the child's parent would fail and that the child's family would further shatter.

Even if nothing direct were said, the child would probably sense the conflicting feelings, and might feel like a pawn in an emotional tug-of-war. At the same time, the foster parent would be caught in a painful double bind, trying dutifully to encourage parent-child progress, but struggling with personal grief at the likely loss of the hoped-for adoption. All these factors explain why prospective foster parents are wisely warned never to consider fostering as a route to adoption, where adoption is the goal.

On the other hand, many children do become available for adoption after months or years in foster care. If such a child is already happily living with a loving family who would gladly make the arrangement permanent, this is often the best possible solution. The natural and loving progression can spare the child the needless trauma of yet another disruption. For this reason, it is perfectly valid, and caring and responsible, to foster parent not with a *goal* of eventually adopting but with a *willingness* to consider it if the need arises.

Because adoption by a former foster parent can be such a good solution for a child, with benefits for the adoptive family as well, it has gained greatly in popularity in recent years. Following formal policies or informal practices, caseworkers in many states actively encourage such adoptions. In New York State, for example, well over half of all children adopted through the state social services department are children adopted by a former foster parent. In some states, such as California, the practice is encouraged by matching, at the time of foster care placement, foster parents who would be willing to adopt with children who are considered likely to become available for adoption.

The Challenge

Perhaps the biggest challenge in maintaining an openness about adoption while fostering is the emotional tug of uncertainty. Your head may know that it is a responsible and appropriate course—indeed, it may well be the *most* supportive of the child's needs—but your heart may ache for certainty one way or the other.

This struggle can be compared to another major form of love: dating and marriage. We all know it is self-defeating to begin every dating relationship with the thought "I hope we'll fall in love and get married." It is far wiser to enjoy the new friendship one day at a time, considering marriage only if and when it becomes a realistic option. Yet most of us have, at some time or other, acted unwisely in love. We may rush a relationship, become too possessive, perhaps even scare the other person away. It takes maturity, a strong sense of self, and a good network of social supports to avoid letting a sense of neediness and urgency dominate our love relationships.

This is equally true in the delicate balance of fostering with a willingness to consider, but not set as a goal, adoption. In fact, this balance is even more important in foster parenting, because the other person affected is not an adult but an already vulnerable child. Additionally, the adoption decision involves more than just the adopter and the adoptee—it also involves the waiver or termination of the birthparent's rights, an agency decision, and a court order.

Even if you are advised that a child you are fostering is likely to become available for adoption—and even if the child seems happy and at home with you—it is wiser and fairer to care for that child one day at a time, without strings attached. And the very same qualities noted above will be key to meeting that challenge: maturity, a strong sense of self, and a good network of social supports.

If you believe you have (and can continue to develop) these strengths, the fostering-to-possible-adoption route may offer a rare opportunity to build a sense of family in a gradual, loving way that responds to the child's actual needs.

Ken Anderson's Family

With all the children in Ken Anderson's life, you might expect him to be hectic and harried. As a younger man, Ken raised five biological sons to adulthood, largely as a single parent. Now, the second time around, he is raising seven children: Taisha and Thomas, the twelve-year-old twins he adopted two years ago; Bobby, the nine-year-old who was his first adoptive child at age five; Nikita and Mona, sisters age seven and three, who are currently in preadoptive placement with Ken; and Michelle and Sherry, two-year-old twins in foster care. Yet, somehow, instead of hectic, he seems warm, gentle, cheerful, and even serene.

Like many, Ken took a roundabout road to the inner peace that seems so much a part of him now. Separated from his own parents as a child, Ken was raised within his closely knit, rural black southern community, largely by relatives and family friends. "I couldn't be with my parents," he explains, "but I always knew there were adults who cared. It might be a neighbor, or someone at church, but I felt like there were folks watching out for me."

Married as a young man, and divorced five children later, Ken found himself prematurely thrust into a primary parental role. Although proud of the job he did, and of the successes his children have achieved, he can hardly describe those years as peaceful or easy. Ken loved his children, but he often felt trapped by the demands on him. When the boys were grown, Ken quickly adopted the lifestyle of a carefree bachelor.

And that might have been the end of the story—until a crisis intervened. Late one evening, Ken surprised a burglar in his home and was shot in the head. First near death, then recuperating, Ken had both the time and the challenge to reflect on what was most important to him in life. It was, he realized, raising children.

Because Ken wanted to make a long-range commitment to second-time parenting, his first thought was to immediately pursue adoption. As he learned more about the needs of children today, however, he decided that another route would be more responsive. He would foster parent, offering care and stability for as long or as short a period as the child needed—but be available to adopt if the child could not go home.

The first three children who came to Ken, and several since, did return to their families of birth. But Bobby's mother, who was ill (and later died), asked Ken to adopt Bobby, and he did so happily. Later, Ken adopted Taisha and Thomas, when their biological parents' parental rights were terminated because they couldn't provide a safe family setting. Although he hopes to adopt Nikita and Mona, whose mother is appealing the termination of her parental rights, Ken has pledged to help them adjust whether they stay with him or return to their mother. The uncertainty is not easy for Ken, but he reasons that he is an adult and they are children, so it is his job to ease the way for them. All of the children's biological parents are made welcome to visit, even after an adoption is complete.

In many ways, Ken has helped to re-create for the children the comforting sense of community that he retained as a child, even when separated from his own parents. Active within a large, closely knit Baptist church in a historical black Washington, D.C., neighborhood, Ken and his second family have forged the bonds of extended family. The three oldest children were baptized together in a festive ceremony that celebrated their commitment as a family as well as to the church, and each has his or her own set of godparents. (Although the younger, nonadopted children were not baptized in that ceremony, out of respect for their still-existing social ties to their family of origin, they were included in the festivities and properly fussed over.) The children all sing in the youth choir and go to the church summer camp. Unlike school, or just about any other setting in today's fast-paced society, there is little pressure to compete or prove themselves within the church family.

"People ask me how I can raise all these children as a single man," says Ken, chuckling. "They have no idea [of] all the women in my church just aching to take care of my 'poor motherless children.' I've got babysitters like you wouldn't believe."

Planning for the children's future is an important part of parental responsibility for Ken, especially in light of their possible medical and other needs. Thanks to carefully drafted adoption agreements, which Ken had reviewed by a lawyer specializing in child welfare issues, all of the children's medical care, mental health, and special education needs are paid for by the state social services department until age eighteen. The family also receives a monthly adoption subsidy for each child, equal in amount to the foster care payments received before the adoptions. This is important because, recognizing his own age and the need to plan for the children's future, Ken puts most of his salary into retirement funds, disability insurance, savings, and annuities—all with survivor's benefits for the children. His will, which he updates with each new adoption, names a family member or godparent as guardian for each child (keeping birthsiblings together), so they would not have to reenter foster care.

Planning for the future also means helping the children prepare to be productive, independent adults. "When my first set of children were growing up," says Ken, "I knew exactly what to tell them about their future. They were going to college. Period. That was their future, and I wasn't going to hear any different. But with my second set, I have to be more individual. Some of them may go to college, some may not be college material. If college isn't realistic, we need to think about other ways they can get marketable skills and be able to take care of themselves.

"At the same time, I try to help them to try everything, to learn what they can be good at. They take piano lessons, tennis lessons, dance lessons, you name it. If I push them, it's not to do this or be that, but to just try, and to take pride in their efforts."

The Logistics

If you are foster parenting a child or children who become available for adoption, there will probably be few formalities in terms of selection and approval. In most states, the same agency that placed the child with you for foster care will facilitate the adoption. If the child is doing well in your care—and, if old enough to express a preference, wants to stay with you—that will usually be persuasive. Most caseworkers will make every effort to encourage and facilitate the adoption, waiving costs and even usual selection criteria if needed.

The adoption process will follow the general steps outlined in the previous chapter, but will probably be somewhat streamlined. The home study document will likely be completed by a caseworker who already knows you, who will probably be especially encouraging, and who may not even need to make extra visits to your home. One or more court hearings will take place, but the court will almost certainly accept the agency's decision as correct, since they have worked with you successfully in the past. Once again, however, the adoption agreement—crucial to safeguarding your child's future security—should be carefully reviewed by your attorney.

Possible Barriers to Post–Foster Care Adoption

Sometimes foster parents can't adopt a child in their care, although the child needs adoption and the foster parents are loving and responsible. Some reasons for this relate to competing concerns about the welfare of the child. If the child does not want the adoption or has not been doing well in the foster home, obviously this could prevent the adoption, even though the foster parents might not be at fault. Also, if the child has relatives who are willing and able to provide a loving home, these relatives may be given preference. (In some states, regulations list both current foster parents and relatives as preferred adopters, and caseworkers must decide on a case-by-case basis when both a relative and a current foster parent seeks to adopt a child or children.) Finally, if the foster parents are of a different race or culture from the child, the agency may try first to find an adoptive home of the child's race or culture, particularly if the child has not been in foster care a long time and/or the foster parents have little contact with people and experiences of the child's heritage.

Some of the most heart-wrenching adoption dilemmas involve foster parents who love and want to adopt a child but are passed over in favor of a relative or family that caseworkers believe is a better match in race, culture, or ability to meet the child's needs. Often there is no easy answer in such cases. If the child is adopted transracially, or by a family that is not best suited to meeting the child's needs, that will create one set of difficulties. If the child is separated from a caring foster family, or made to wait a long time while a more optimal match is sought, that, too, will be hard on the child.

If this happens within your family, try to avoid a hard-line position that could force the issue. Talk to those responsible for making the decision, really trying to listen and to consider what is best for the child. At the same time, express any concerns you may have, and be frank about your feelings for the child and your impressions as to the child's needs.

You may want to emphasize your interest in staying available to the child in whatever capacity is needed. In many cases, it is possible to work out a positive arrangement that will allow the child to remain warmly connected to both the former foster parents and to relatives or adopters of the child's culture. If tempers mount, however, a cooperative, nurturing solution becomes less and less likely. You could find yourself permanently separated from a child for whom you could have remained, at a minimum, a caring friend.

Outdated Policies

A possible barrier still occurring, but in a decreasing number of cases, is that a few offices continue to follow outdated policies that disqualify current or former foster parents as adopters. Based on the idea that foster parents who aren't barred from future adoption might undermine efforts to reunify children with their parents, this once common policy has generally been replaced by a more flexible approach to meeting children's actual needs. It occasionally surfaces in formal or informal policies, however.

You can follow an appeals process to contest any such policies, which discriminate against a group of people who may be uniquely well situated to nurture the children in their care. If internal appeals are unsuccessful, you may want to consider consulting an attorney specializing in child welfare issues to contest the counterproductive policy.

When a Child Lingers in Foster Care

Another problem may relate to bureaucratic overload. It is a sad fact that, largely because of underfunding and overcrowded caseloads, and partially because of management errors, many children remain in foster care long after any realistic hope for return to their parents has ended. If this happens to a child in your care, you may recognize that the child is in need of permanence, and be happy to provide it—but legally the child is not free to be adopted. This leaves both you and the child in limbo, never really certain whether you are a permanent family.

If return to the parent is truly unrealistic, the obvious solution is for the agency to seek parental consent for an adoption. If the parent(s) do not consent, the agency could then seek a court-ordered termination of parental rights so that the child can be adopted.

Your problem, however, is an even more delicate one. If the agency does not act, what can and should you do?

Be aware that the folks you may be thinking about prodding to act are the same folks who will report to the judge on who would make the best adoptive parent. If you create the impression that you are more concerned with your needs than the child's, that could fairly and reasonably be reported as a negative factor. If you hurt and anger caseworkers by making them look bad, that probably shouldn't be a part of their decisions or affect their reports—but caseworkers are only human, and, realistically, it may.

Another reason you'll want to tread carefully is that you really aren't impartial, and it is often hard to know what is right. For example, it is natural to feel angry and frustrated with the child's parent(s) at times, and to conclude that it would be best for the child if they would just disappear. For example, a parent may complete a drug treatment program, then return to drug use, utterly disappointing the child. You may conclude that the situation is hopeless, and possibly you are right. Yet many ex-addicts kicked their habits only after a few or even several tries. The severing of the parent-child relationship is a serious step, and may be a blow for the child more serious than waiting. If you and the caseworker see the child's needs and the parent's potential differently, it may be very difficult to know who is right.

There are no easy solutions, but options do exist. If you already have a good relationship with the child's caseworker, that may be the logical place to start.

Under the federal Child Welfare and Adoption Act, every child in foster care must have a permanency plan. Ask about the child's permanency plan and whether the goal is adoption.

If you don't believe the current permanency plan is in tune with the realistic situation and the child's actual needs, express your concerns. Rather than focusing on what the caseworker or the agency's lawyers should be doing, however, you may want to emphasize ways in which you would be happy to help: to adopt the child, if needed; to testify in court, if useful; to facilitate postadoption visits by the parent, if appropriate; and so on.

Most caseworkers want to perform their jobs well, but often find it difficult to do much more than meet the most immediate crises. By offering to help reach a permanent solution, you may help the agency move beyond the daily bandaging.

A second option is to find out if an attorney, a guardian ad litem, or a court appointed special advocate (known by the acronym CASA) is representing the child. If so, in most states that person will also have the right to petition the court for a termination of parental rights so that the child can be adopted—and may have more time than the agency to do so. You might invite that person to visit the child at your house, then mention your concerns for the child's permanency.

Even then, choose your words carefully to avoid seeming to criticize anyone involved. That you must be so carefully political just to bring attention to a child's needs is a shame, but it may be necessary. The child's advocate can be a very important player—and a wonderful ally—in determining the child's future.

Your final option is to seek help from an attorney of your own who is experienced in child welfare law. Choose someone who is used to working closely with the agency's lawyers and the child's advocate, and whose personality is effective but not abrasive. This last point cannot be expressed too strongly, because the truth is that, in most states, you have very limited rights in the matter. Decisions will be—and should be—made based on the needs of the child.

An abrasive, aggressive, or inexperienced lawyer who

barges into court and demands your "rights" will only succeed in alienating just about everyone involved. A persuasive negotiator, however, may help the others to see you as a permanent resource for the child, then offer to do the work (while tactfully giving everyone else the credit). If it succeeds in safeguarding the future of a child you love, that is all that matters.

As you explore these various options, keep in mind that adoption is not the only method for establishing a more permanent bond with a child. In many cases, permanent guardianship may be an equally sound route, may be less difficult legally to accomplish, and may not require the complete termination of parental rights. Since the exact legal status and impact of guardianship varies by state, you should discuss and compare it carefully with your lawyer.

The Newly Committed Family

The transition from fostering to adoption or guardianship is, for many families, one of the most moving milestones in their shared family life. Like marriage, it expresses a lifetime commitment to care for another person, in sickness and in health, in good times and in bad. Also like marriage, it builds on and deepens an already existing relationship. Yet in many ways this commitment is even more profound, because the responsibility is to a dependent child. Spouses may divorce, but your child remains your child.

Like every other family, the postfostering adoptive family will have its ups and downs. One of the greatest satisfactions will be the sense of having built an intentional family and watching it grow and mature in love and hope. One of the greatest challenges may be struggling with recurring anxieties.

Your newly adoptive child may act out at times, testing to see if the commitment is really there. The teen years, often rocky in all types of families, may reawaken the child's early angers and fears of abandonment. You in turn may have moments of despair, wondering if you did the right thing. Try to remember that you are not alone, that your feelings are natural, and that others share both your joys and your concerns.

If you ask Ken Anderson whether he is happy within his family, you'll quickly realize that, although his answer is basically positive, the question is too simplistic. "When I was a younger man," he says, "happiness was always my goal. But what kind of a goal is that? You're happy one day; you've reached your goal. The next day a problem comes up and you're unhappy. You've lost your goal. So you're letting outside events define whether or not you've reached your goal.

"Now I see that acceptance is the goal. Accepting life and finding contentment within it. Loving your children every day, whether or not they behave lovably on any given day. And, with that acceptance, I find myself more content now than I've ever been in my life."

Seven

INTERNATIONAL ADOPTION

International adoption is a very good alternative for many children without parents in their own countries. Where there's a shortage of potential adopters in the child's country of origin, international adoption may be the child's best chance for a permanent family.

—Robin Allen
The Barker Foundation

International adoption—the adoption of children from other countries—soared during the 1980s. More recently, it tapered off, as some nations, and some potential adopters, saw that it has both advantages and disadvantages.

Unlike other forms of adoption, for which no centralized statistics are kept, the surge in international adoption can be documented. In 1980, just over 5,000 foreign-born children were adopted by U.S. citizens. By 1987, that annual total had reached a peak of 10,000, from which it has since slightly declined.

Nearly all children adopted internationally are from developing nations, where poverty is common. Most were abandoned at birth or in early childhood and placed into orphanages or other institutional care, rather than family foster care. Very few are newborns, but many are quite young. For example, the typical child placed by the Barker Foundation, a Washington, D.C., private adoption agency specializing in international adoptions, is three to five months old and was born in a hospital.

Even children identified for adoption at birth may be several months old by the time the adoption is complete, simply because the adoption requirements imposed by both the American and host country governments are complex. There may be a wait of months before an international adoptee is cleared to come to the United States for adoption.

Adoption of a child from another country involves several challenges not found in the adoption of American-born children. These range from finding the right adoption agency, to completing complex paperwork, to addressing the cultural needs of children from another country and culture. It is also quite expensive, typically costing from $7,000 to $18,000.

International adoption seems to be particularly attractive to many middle- or upper-income European American couples, seeking very young children without severe physical or emotional challenges, who are open to and interested in children of other cultures. They cite as advantages that international adoption often involves much less of a wait than adopting an infant without known disabilities through an agency, and that it may be less expensive than many identified adoptions. It may also lead to the adoption of a child who is younger than many children currently awaiting adoption in the United States. Additionally, many people who adopt internationally seem genuinely drawn by the intercultural aspect, which can be exciting and enriching.

A Child within a Year

Peggy and Tom Dean adopted their son Matt, a Korean child, through a Virginia-based international adoption agency. They were drawn to the agency after learning that they'd be able to adopt fairly quickly, in contrast to the long waits expected at many local agencies placing American-born children. That Peggy has a sister who was adopted from China was an added incentive.

The northern Virginia couple applied to the agency in November 1988, received an intake interview in January 1989, and had their home study done nine months later. One month after the home study, the Deans saw their first picture of the child they would adopt. Four months later, six-month-old Matt was in their arms. Their total wait: about a year—at a time when a nearby agency placing U.S.-born children wasn't even taking names for its adoption waiting list.

Race and Culture

Many of the rewards and challenges facing someone who adopts a foreign-born child arise from the fact that the child will be different, both in appearance and in his or her cultural roots. Once many people believed that a child adopted into the United States came as a clean slate, to be imprinted solely with American culture, his or her ethnicity and heritage ignored. Now child development experts understand that a child's biological identity and heritage are crucial to the child's sense of identity and self-esteem.

Besides, most internationally adopted children are not infants. Even at as young as a year, they already have the beginnings of language and culture as a part of their life experience. They have already lost their first families and first homes; they should not have to lose, too, the comfort of cultural ties.

Sensitive adoptive parents realize that children adopted from other lands need to have their differences recognized and appreciated. Although they gave their Korean child an American name, Peggy and Tom Dean say they've been trying to help Matt connect with his culture. At sixteen months of age, Matt received from Peggy the traditional kimonolike outfit worn by Korean children. They have gone to parties sponsored by the adoption agency so that he could meet other Korean-born adoptees. Happily, children's books are now reflecting greater cultural diversity than ever before, and Peggy and Tom have found books of Korean and other Asian fairy tales to read to Matt.

The adoption agencies involved in international placements tend to question potential adopters closely regarding their attitudes about race and ethnicity. If you are interested in international adoption, you should do the same of yourself. Ask yourself how you feel about racial differences. Your family is about to become multiracial; are you prepared to ensure that the culture of all family members is shared and respected? Will you feel any different when your child becomes a tall and darker-than-you teen, possibly—hopefully—with some tall and darker-than-you friends? Keep in mind that a young child who does not seem to care about race and ethnicity will often become much more interested and concerned about ethnic identity as a teen or young adult.

How will you deal with that segment of the public that is not open-minded about race and that may, at minimum, treat your multiracial family as a curiosity? American adopters, while in stores or out for walks, often encounter neighbors or strangers who can't resist staring or even pointing out how their foreign child has such cute dark hair, such sweet slanty eyes, such a round face. Peggy Dean says she has even been asked, "Is he yours?" or "How cute! Where did you get him?"

Some people will tell you, sometimes in earshot of the child, that your foreign adoption makes you a living saint. (No one should choose any form of adoption to help save the world. You do it to love a child.)

Racist attitudes in the world around you may become increasingly problematic when the youth reaches the teen years and adulthood. Some interracial and intercultural families have been shocked to find their friends and neighbors, whose children always played happily with theirs, reacting adversely when the childhood friendships progress to teen dating.

No doubt about it, to be different in America is to draw attention and even racism. The question is, can you handle it? And how will you help your foreign-born child to understand it, while maintaining the child's sense of personal and cultural pride?

For some families, the challenges are as much internal

as external. Most adoptive families, recognizing the importance of ethnic identity to their children, do try to encourage at least some level of intercultural involvement. Yet truly sharing the child's culture almost certainly requires forming friendships with adults of that culture, and not everyone has good cross-cultural skills.

Additionally, celebrating the child's biological heritage means daily acknowledging a difference, a major way in which your family differs from families formed by birth. This may be difficult and even painful, particularly if you remain saddened by the loss of the birth experience.

An International Family

Despite the challenges, many families do enjoy the cultural richness of international adoption. For Gail Haley and Fred Grandy of Cambridge, Massachusetts, who spent a year living in Ecuador when they were first married, the adoption of an Ecuadorian child a few years later seemed only natural. To make it happen, Gail, who is an educator, arranged a vaguely work-related trip back to the city where they had lived, and visited an orphanage to meet and choose a child. Six months, a second trip, and pounds of paperwork later, they had a one-year-old daughter.

Their daughter had been named Maria by her birthmother, and that, as far as Gail and Fred were concerned, was and is her name. Maria will learn English first, but they plan to seek a Spanish-speaking day-care provider and enroll Maria in a bilingual kindergarten and grade school. Moving to the suburbs, by the way, is out, since the Cambridge public school system offers an unusual bilingual program designed for children whose first language is either English or Spanish. But that is fine with them, since they have always thrived on the intercultural aspect of the life of their city.

Choices about Names

The different decisions that the adoptive parents of Maria and Matt made about names highlight the important question of whether to reflect the culture of the child's birth in his or her name. For Maria's parents, the choice was clear: she already had a name and (for the reasons discussed in Chapter 2) they respected it. Matt was adopted in infancy, however, and the parents chose a name from their own families of birth. The issue may also come up even with older children, as parents decide whether to use an Americanized nickname, such as "Joey" for "José," or "Bob" for "Roberto."

If you adopt a child from another country, even as an infant, you may want to consider retaining a previously chosen name that reflects the child's culture of origin. Doing so is a powerful statement of respect for that culture, and of your willingness to recognize and enjoy ways that your child is different from you. At the same time, as Matt's parents demonstrate, there are other ways to convey that message as well.

The question of whether to use an Americanized nickname can be decided by the child. A good time to raise this might be when the child begins first grade, saying, for example, "Roberto is a lovely name, and is common in Guatemala, where you were born. Some people find Bobby a fun nickname, and easier to say. Which would you like people to call you at school?"

Some parents worry that the child will not be well accepted with a foreign name, but this is less often a problem than feared. If acceptance problems do arise, they likely reflect a deeper problem of social intolerance, and will not be solved by a name change. In fact, urging the child to use an Americanized name in response may suggest to the child that conformity is the best approach—a message both unaffirming and, if the child appears physically different from classmates, impossible. A better response to any concerns over local intolerance would be to become involved in community education and/or to seek out a more diverse and inclusive community.

The International Adoption Process

International adoption is generally accomplished in a manner very similar to that used for the adoption of American-born children, but with an added layer of complexity. Most people adopt through a private agency that specializes in international adoption. It may be a U.S. agency or one in the country in which an adoption is desired.

Adopting through a U.S. Agency

The least difficult and least risky route to adopting internationally is through a U.S. agency specializing in international adoption. Such agencies have associates they trust and regularly work with in one or more nations, and they can assist you through every step of the process, from application to postadoption support services. This was the route followed by Peggy and Tom Dean in adopting their child from Korea. A couple discussed later in this chapter also used this method to adopt a Thai child.

The international adoption process "can be cumbersome, unpredictable, and confusing," observes Robin Allen of the Barker Foundation. "People tend to need a local adoption agency, because they're dealing with bureaucracies in two countries."

International adoption through an agency typically follows the steps discussed in detail in Chapter 5. The major differences are cost, additional paperwork, possible travel required, and cultural aspects.

Adopting Directly through an Agency in the Other Country

Another, more challenging route is to deal directly with an adoption agency in the country in which you hope to adopt. This choice requires that you have sufficient time for the necessary foreign trips, and that the organization you are working with overseas is competent and reliable. It is also helpful, and may even be necessary, for you to be fluent in that nation's language. This was the method used by Gail Haley and Fred Grandy, discussed earlier, in adopting their daughter Maria from Ecuador.

Although the logistics are difficult, most foreign adoption agencies are trustworthy. They are often regulated by their nation's government and may be cautious about creating a situation that might harm their reputation or that of their government. Many such organizations are delighted to be dealing with adoptive parents whom they can interview in person and who speak the language of their future child. They will not, however, be able to provide the ongoing postadoptive support services that a U.S. agency could. Additionally, international travel is very likely to be necessary.

Some people choose to work directly with a foreign agency because they do not meet an adoption requirement of local agencies, such as maximum age limits. Be aware, though, that the foreign agency will have its own criteria, which may be as restrictive as many U.S. agencies—or even more so. Some foreign agencies, for example, require that the adopters be Christians. At least one South Korean agency refuses to work with adopters who are obese.

The foreign agency may require participation by a U.S. agency as well, especially in completing the home study. You may also want to turn to a local agency for services that a foreign agency cannot provide, such as postplacement counseling.

Use of an Attorney or Other Facilitator

Most risky of all the routes to international adoption is the use of a third party, whether an attorney or "adoption facilitator," either in the United States or in the foreign nation, as a substitute for working with an agency. Too many cases have been reported of prospective adopters giving such individuals thousands of dollars, only to see them disappear with the cash or renege on their offer.

Even more disturbing is the possibility that an adoption facilitator could be engaged in the profitable enterprise of paying low-income mothers to part with their infants. A Maryland couple, Howard and Cathy Burton, said they were in contact with a Los Angeles woman who claimed to be the local agent for Latin American adoptions. As they worked with her, they noted that every child she referred to them for adoption was currently living with his or her mother. When pressed for more details as to why the children were being placed, the facilitator clammed up. Wisely, from an ethical and emotional point of view, they rejected the referrals and stopped working with the facilitator.

Although many reputable attorneys work in international adoption, they generally—and more appropriately—work on the legal tasks and leave to agencies the actual screening, placement, and adoption services. After all, even the most skilled attorney is not in a position to offer the adoption preparation and matching, and the pre- and post-adoptive services necessary for the child and family. Your best bet is to seek an attorney experienced in the legal process of international adoption—and preferably one recommended by the agency with which you are working—and have that person work in cooperation with the agency.

Setbacks You May Encounter

Even when you deal with a completely trustworthy agency and attorney, foreign adoption may still have setbacks and risks. Some of the risks arise because national governments are indirectly involved. Howard and Cathy Burton, for instance, were still in the process (when this book went to press) of attempting to adopt a Peruvian child. They had met the child and spent first a week, then later a month with him in Peru, but the process dragged on for months. An early setback occurred because the Peruvian government attorney handling the adoption paperwork had too large a backlog of cases. Later, government concerns over an alleged baby selling scandal caused adoptions nationwide to be suspended.

Other nations, like Peru, have at times responded to child welfare or political concerns by suddenly suspending foreign adoptions. The U.S. government has also occasionally responded to cases of alleged baby selling in foreign nations by refusing to grant entry visas to children being adopted by Americans in those nations. In 1991, for example, reports of baby selling in Rumania prompted the U.S. government to temporarily stop issuing visas for Rumanian children who were being adopted in Rumania by U.S. citizens. A number of newly formed families were left stranded in Rumania until the matter was resolved.

Travel Requirements

You may, particularly in South American or Eastern European adoptions, need to travel to the child's country to complete the adoption and take your child into your care. Completing the adoption may also require you to stay for several days to process paperwork. Of course, you could certainly use the opportunity to take an extended vacation, learning about the culture that brought you your child.

When adopting from a country with long-established

relations with U.S. adoption agencies, most notably Korea, an overseas trip is much less likely to be needed. Since you would still have to pay for someone to escort the child to the United States—and, again, to see and learn about your child's nation of origin—you may want to go there and bring the child home.

Paperwork

International adoption requires quite a bit of special paperwork—in addition to, not instead of, the papers you'd complete for a U.S. adoption.

For the Immigration and Naturalization Service

The major piece of immigration paperwork is form I-600, the "Petition to Classify Orphan as an Immediate Relative," which you must file with the Immigration and Naturalization Service (INS). The I-600 is currently required, although it may be replaced by another form in the future.

The I-600 requires you to show that the child you are adopting is, as legally defined by federal legislation, an "orphan." The legal definition of orphan includes children who have been abandoned by their parents or whose parents have died. A child still with a parent may also be an orphan, but only if just one parent is still present, can't care for the child, and wants to have the child adopted. A child with two parents still available would not be considered an orphan, even if both parents wished to place the child for adoption.

Official documents needed to classify a child as an orphan may include a signed release from the caregiving parent, placing the child for adoption and certifying that the other parent is dead or has abandoned the child. If the child was in an orphanage, a statement from the orphanage must certify how the child came to be an orphan and that the child is free for adoption. These documents must be translated into English.

Along with form I-600, you must provide proof of U.S. citizenship, a copy of your home study, proof of marriage (and of divorce, if this is the case), and several sets of fingerprints. The fingerprints of you and your spouse can be taken by your local police department or by the INS.

You also must show proof that you are adopting the child, which is generally furnished by the agency with which you are working. If your home state has special requirements for adoption, you must show that you have met them.

Once your child arrives in the United States, he or she will be considered a resident alien until naturalization is completed. As long as your child remains an alien, you will need to inform the INS of your new address whenever you move. To complete the child's naturalization, you will have additional paperwork to complete and submit to the INS over time.

For the Other Nation

The nation whose citizen you are adopting will also require a variety of documents. At a minimum, most nations require a certified copy of your home study, and your birth and marriage certificates. In general, these must be translated into the host country's language and are filed with that nation's consular office in the United States. Some countries, including most in Latin America, require that all documents be notarized, and that the notary's seal and signature be certified as valid by the county that issued the seal.

If you are working through a U.S. adoption agency, your local agency should assist you in identifying and completing the paperwork required by the other government. If you are adopting directly through an agency in another country, an attorney specializing in international adoption can advise you on what paperwork that nation will require.

For Your State

Some states require that, at the time you bring the child you plan to adopt into the country and your state, you supply the state with a copy of the child's birth certificate, as well as a copy of your home study. Some also require some proof that you can afford to care for the child. Wisconsin, for instance, requires the posting of a $1,000 bond.

Health Concerns

Foreign children being adopted usually come from developing nations where medical care is limited and low-level chronic illnesses are widespread. For instance, in recent years most children from developing Asian nations, such as Thailand or Vietnam, carried Hepatitis B. If left untreated, this could be transmitted to unvaccinated members of the adoptive family, even if it had not made the child visibly ill. A recent cholera epidemic in parts of Latin America has also raised concerns. Other children have been so malnourished as to be developmentally delayed.

If you adopt internationally, you need to be aware of these health factors. Your child should have a complete physical and dental exam as soon as possible after arriving in this country, and receive all medical services needed.

Children with Special Needs

Some children available for adoption internationally have mild to serious special physical or mental disabilities. Because of the general poverty of many developing nations, the fate of these children, if not adopted, is particularly bleak. They will likely not receive the medical and psychological treatment that could be made available to them in the United States, and they may not be well accepted in their own country. Adoption by a U.S. citizen can provide such a child with a much better life.

If you decide to adopt a foreign-born child with special needs, however, you'll need to plan and consider carefully. You cannot be assured of publicly provided medical coverage or adoption subsidies, as you could if you were adopting a U.S. child with special needs. You need to evaluate carefully whether you'll be able to afford needed care, and whether your family health care coverage will cover your adoptive child for preexisting conditions. Also try to gather information in advance about free or low-cost services available through your state social services and vocational rehabilitation departments.

Unfortunately, in making your decisions, you cannot assume that you will have full information. As discussed in earlier chapters, there is always a risk that young children may have undiagnosed needs and disabilities. Accurate diagnosis may be especially difficult in the international adoption context, since many children have not had good medical care and screening in the past. There is no evidence to suggest, however, that children adopted internationally are any more likely than U.S. adoptees to have serious special needs, and most, in fact, do not. The important point is that you must, as always, be prepared to adopt with full commitment to whatever the child's needs turn out to be.

Friendship and Support

Families who adopt internationally can especially benefit from alliances with others who share their experiences. As with any form of adoption, a good place to start is the local adoptive parents' organization. Your local chapter of any adoptive parents' group will typically have members who have adopted internationally. International families may have their own subgroup within the local chapter.

At least two adoptive parents' groups emphasize international adoption. The Latin American Parents Association focuses on those who adopt from that region. Adoptive Families of America publishes the magazine *OURS* and has several support groups of international adopters nationwide. Both are listed in the appendix.

Becoming an Intercultural Family

Mary and Dan Phelps, a Madison, Wisconsin, couple, had their first child biologically, and decided by choice to seek a second child by adoption. They hoped for an infant, but learned that—in addition to requiring a long wait for a U.S. infant—many local agencies required that adopters be infertile.

They decided to consider international adoption, but again encountered limitations. They are over age forty and not Christian, factors which disqualified them with an agency placing South Korean children. Working through Holt International Children's Services, an international adoption agency in Eugene, Oregon, the couple settled on Thailand, which has had on-again, off-again cycles of foreign adoption, and was currently permitting children to be adopted overseas.

The couple's home study was done by a local social service agency. They sent it to Holt along with several letters of recommendation, including some written by Thai friends in Thai. Eventually, they were matched with a two-year-old boy, Kim—the earliest age, they were told, at which Thai children are available for overseas adoption. Mary and Dan were required to fly to Thailand to meet Kim and bring him home. To their delight, they found that the orphanage, like many in that relatively prosperous developing nation, was a pleasant place, with its own educational enrichment program.

When Dan and Mary brought Kim back to the States, a medical checkup brought more good news: the child's only physical problem was a few cavities. Good medical care at the orphanage had kept the child from infections common to Asia, including Hepatitis B.

Two years later, Mary says their family life is now interwoven with a connection to Thai culture. Kim plays with Thai toys, speaks a few Thai words, and enjoys his mother's regular forays into Thai cooking. Madison is a college town, and Mary often takes Kim to events sponsored by the Thai students' association. The family plans to travel to Thailand someday.

Not all foreign adoptions are so relatively free of complications, but many are happy and enriching. By using reputable agencies and an experienced attorney, you can minimize the most common setbacks. By making an extra effort to embrace not only a child but your child's culture, you can help build a family in which cultural differences are appreciated, enjoyed, and celebrated.

Eight

IDENTIFIED ADOPTION

Identified adoption offers an important option for couples or singles wanting to adopt, and for birth-parents wanting to place their child for adoption. By opening up the process, it offers a different set of benefits than confidential adoption does, which may better meet some families' needs.

—Dawn Smith-Pliner
Friends in Adoption

Long before adoption agencies existed, parents who could not care for their children (or, in the case of unmarried mothers, who were socially forbidden to do so) quietly made private arrangements with others to have their child adopted. Although many of these arrangements were never legalized, others were. Parents could, and can to this day, consent to their children's adoption by specific named persons. When made official by a judge, the adoption is as complete and final as one arranged through an agency.

Identified adoption is a modern twist on this very traditional idea. At its most basic, identified adoption consists of (1) an agreement between specific birthparent(s) and specific adoptive parent(s) for a child to be adopted, and (2) a court order legalizing the adoption.

In general, to assist the judge in determining whether the adoption is in the child's best interests, a home study of the prospective adopters, by a licensed adoption agency or a court-affiliated family service program, is also needed and legally required. In most states, however, the home study may occur either before or after the birthparent physically places the child with the prospective adopters.

Within this broad definition of identified adoption lie many variations. Entirely private arrangements between family members or friends who knew each other prior to the child's conception now constitute only a small percentage of identified adoptions. Today most identified adoptions involve a pregnant woman and an adopting couple who, although unacquainted before the pregnancy, find each other through advertising, an attorney specializing in identified adoption, or an adoption agency assisting or specializing in identified adoption. Usually, the child is adopted soon after birth.

Some identified adoptions involve a high degree of openness and exchange between the birth- and adoptive parents. Some even result in an open adoption, with continuing contact between the child and the birthparents. Others involve only a very structured, limited exchange; for example, preadoption phone conversations and exchange of written materials only, and no postadoption contact until the child reaches adulthood.

You may have heard identified adoption referred to as "independent adoption." That term can be confusing, however, since identified adoption is not really independent, as anyone who undertakes it quickly learns. The process requires a great deal of interaction and cooperation with many parties, including at least one lawyer, the social worker who does your home study, and, of course, the child's parents of origin. Nonetheless, the term "independent adoption" may be used to describe a specific type of identified adoption, in which the prospective adopters find the parents, make an agreement, and physically take the child into their care—all before contacting any agency to do a home study. These privately arranged placements are the most controversial form of identified adoption, as will be discussed later in the chapter. In fact, they are opposed by the Child Welfare League of America and are illegal in at least five states.

Identified adoption, although often associated with placements arranged outside of adoption agencies, is increasingly being facilitated by agencies as well. The first step in a typical agency-based identified adoption will be the home study process, just as discussed in Chapter 5. Once approved, however, the adopters may begin immediately to seek a pregnant woman interested in placing her child, after birth, for adoption. If all parties agree, that placement may then be made through the agency, with the agency facilitating information exchanges and perhaps even a meeting. This form of identified adoption is legal in every state.

The Identified Adoption Process

An important feature of most identified adoptions is the agreement between the pregnant woman, the child's father (if identified and participating), and the prospective adopters. Designed to help promote a healthy pregnancy and childbirth, and to facilitate an adoption after the birth, the agreement does not, however, guarantee that the adoption will actually occur.

According to those who work in the field, the typical woman placing her child through identified adoption is in her early twenties, and has both a high school education and a job. In general, however, she does not have adequate resources for a healthy pregnancy without financial support. For this reason, most identified adoption agreements include the promise by the potential adopters to pay certain medical and living expenses during the pregnancy.

You may hear the pregnant woman in a planned identified adoption referred to as "the birthmother," even before the adoption occurs, but this is inaccurate and could cause misunderstanding. Until the day the woman gives birth, she is, quite simply, a pregnant woman. When she gives birth, she is the child's mother. She becomes the "birthmother," and the adoptive parents become "the mother" and "the father" only if and when the adoption is complete. This language is important to recognizing, respecting, and accepting the pregnant woman's right to change her mind at any time before the final adoption.

This right of the woman to change her mind is not affected by any expenses paid by the prospective adopters during her pregnancy. Although a lawyer representing the adopters (and often a separate lawyer for the pregnant woman and her partner, if any) put the parties' obligations to each other into a written agreement, this doesn't guarantee that an adoption will occur. Rather, the agreement is only a promise by the adopters to pay expenses and an expression of good faith intent by the pregnant woman to place the child for adoption.

If you enter such an agreement, you will probably be asked to pay many expenses associated with the pregnancy and the childbirth, such as the woman's living expenses during the pregnancy, prenatal care, hospitalization, and delivery. Additional expenses may include the cost of any counseling she may need to make her final decision, and her legal costs, if she chooses to consult a lawyer. The total expenses related to the mother and child generally range from about $5,000 to $15,000—not including your own costs related to actually completing the adoption, such as your own attorney's fee, the cost of your home study, your advertising and phone costs, and your travel expenses if the child is born in another state.

You would probably pay at least some expenses related to the child's birth if you were adopting an infant through a confidential, agency-based adoption, but only if and when you actually adopted the child. The adopters' costs in an identified adoption may also be higher because pregnant women using identified adoption may plan ahead and seek the arrangement sooner, thus needing financial support for a longer period of time. (Some women who place their child through a confidential, agency-based adoption wait to do so until after the child is born.) The early contact and your provision of medical and living expenses in an identified adoption may add expense, but it can help encourage a healthy pregnancy and birth.

After the child is born, the biological mother and, if known and participating, the father may sign a consent to adoption, waiving all their parental rights. This opens the door to complete the adoption. The adoption process will involve, as discussed in Chapter 5, a home study, the bringing home of the child, and the legal process. Ways in which these steps may differ in an identified adoption, as well as other features specific to identified adoptions, will be discussed here.

One Family's Experience

The story of Kay and Ira Cohen, a Boston-area couple in their late thirties, and their child shows just how fast identified adoption can occur. Since Massachusetts is one of the six states that do not permit privately arranged preadoption placement, the Cohens worked through a local adoption agency primarily serving Jewish families and children.

As in a traditional agency adoption, the Cohens first went through a home study process and were approved to adopt. There, however, the traditional handling ended. Since the Cohens wanted an infant, and none was available in the near future through the agency, they were promptly referred to a list of lawyers specializing in helping couples find prospective birthparents. In other words, the agency's role in approving the Cohens to adopt was real, but its role in placement was largely on paper. Finding the child was up to the Cohens.

Ira and Kay chose several lawyers from the list and sent them a fax of a letter to be sent to pregnant women considering adoption. The letter described the Cohens and explained why they felt they would make good parents. That was on a Friday; on Monday, they were called by a lawyer in Kansas City about a pregnant woman who was seeking a Jewish couple and liked their letter. After several telephone calls and an in-person meeting, the woman decided they would be her child's parents.

Six months later, the woman went into labor and the Cohens flew to Kansas City. The next morning they were holding a newborn baby boy. The day after that, they were appointed his temporary guardians. (This was unusually quick.) They returned to Massachusetts, where the adoption was finalized a few months later. In less time than it would have taken to gestate one, Kay and Ira had a baby.

Kay and Ira particularly appreciated the interpersonal nature of their adoption, which involved them closely with the birthmother and the birth.

"We wanted a sense of the birthmother," explains Kay, "who she is and what she's like. Our son is going to have a lot of questions about the adoption someday, and we're glad to have a personal sense of his birthmother we can share."

Advantages of Identified Adoption

The popularity of identified adoption has grown in recent years. In part this may be because many adopters, as well as many birthparents, like the person-to-person contact and making their own decision. Identified adoption may also appeal to those who want a closer relationship with their child's birthparents, or at least to gain enough information about them to help the child make peace with his or her own adoption. According to Betty Jean Lifton, author of *Lost & Found: The Adoption Experience*, one of the best means for an adopted child to overcome some of adoption's emotional challenges is for that child to have in-depth information about his or her birthparents. Although identified adoption is not the only way to meet this goal, it certainly provides many opportunities to do so.

Another reason for identified adoption's growing appeal is its reputation as a quick, if expensive, way to adopt an infant. In California, for instance, infants accounted for only 9 percent of all agency adoptions in 1990, but 70 percent of all identified adoptions. And because identified adopters often help with pregnancy and prenatal care costs, the child may have a healthier start.

As Ira and Kay found, identified adoption sometimes happens very rapidly. One early survey of 102 identified adopters found that the majority adopted within four months of beginning their search—and twelve adopted within one month. More typical today is a wait of eight to eighteen months. Of course, since the surveys cover only successful adopters, they don't provide information about those who have not been able to adopt through this route, or who are still searching.

Identified adoption may also attract some people who believe—probably inaccurately—that it is a more promising route for those who are nontraditional adopters, such as singles or significantly older couples. The adopters, however, must still win the confidence of the pregnant woman, who may be traditional in her views. And given the surge in interest in identified adoption, birthparents can be very choosy—probably more so than an agency. As one young woman said, "If I wanted my child to be raised by a single parent, I'd raise him myself. I want him to have more advantages than I could give him, more even than I had myself."

Birthparents also have reasons to find identified adoption attractive. They can choose their child's future parents and have the reassurance of knowing a bit about them. They can know, too, that eliminating the need for foster care will minimize the number of moves and disruptions the child will face. The financial supports provided during pregnancy and childbirth may also be an important and much-needed feature for many young pregnant women.

Finally, both birthparents and adoptive parents may feel more empowered through the personal decision-making process involved in the adoption agreement. Even if they respect the ability of professional social workers to make certain decisions well, they may feel better being a part of all decisions.

Controversy and Risks

Despite its many adherents, identified adoption is not without controversy. Some of the risks are part of every identified adoption. Others exist only in identified adoptions that are not facilitated through an agency.

Identified adoption, by its very nature, involves a practical risk that you must be willing to accept. When you agree to supply medical care and living expenses to a pregnant woman, she agrees that she *intends* to offer the child to you for adoption. Emotionally, however, she can decide for certain only after the child is born, when she signs or chooses not to sign the adoption consent form. The law supports her in this and will not allow her to be coerced into the adoption. Nor will it require the past support, which legally has the status of a gift, to be repaid. This is true no matter how the original legal agreement is drafted, and there is a good reason for it: for the protection of children, the payment of money can't dictate an adoption, nor can mothers be required to give up their children to pay a debt.

Although comparatively few pregnant women reportedly change their minds—and fewer still are suspected of bad faith or insincere original intention—be aware that this risk is part and parcel of identified adoption. You could end up financially supporting the gestation and birth of a child whom you ultimately are not able to adopt and in whose life you will have no further role.

Even when the adoption process goes smoothly, identified adoption tends to be extremely expensive. Including the adopters' own expenses and those of the birthmother, identified adoption typically costs the adopters between $10,000 to $25,000—the broad range reflecting the fact that actual costs are often difficult to predict or control. For many people, this alone is a major disadvantage to identified adoption. Some child advocates worry that the system causes infants to go only to the wealthiest adopters—or to families whose ability to care for them has just been compromised by the incredible expense of the adoption.

Even some people who have successfully and happily completed an identified adoption express concern over costs and the difficulty in controlling them. In their identified adoption, for instance, Ira and Kay Cohen paid for the birthmother's car repairs, new tires, and even cable TV bills. Although they questioned the costs, they feared alienating the woman by objecting. Ultimately, the adoption cost about $17,000, including $2,500 in fees to a lawyer in Kansas and $1,500 to another lawyer in Massachusetts.

Some people also question whether pregnant women considering identified adoption have enough opportunity to obtain counseling, since they may not be working directly with a social services agency. You should be aware, though, that it is in your own best interest—besides being the decent and fair thing to do—to encourage any counseling the woman needs or wants, and to pay the cost if necessary. Adequate counseling can help her to be sure of her decision—an important factor, since she can reverse her decision at any time up to the final adoption. In some states, she may even be able to retract her decision for a brief period after the adoption, particularly if there is evidence that she was denied needed counseling.

Concerns are also raised regarding attorneys with questionable ethical practices. High fees have been reported, for example, in cases where the attorney has preidentified a pregnant woman willing to place her child for adoption. Baby selling is illegal, but it is hard to prove that an inflated fee was influenced by the availability of the baby to be adopted. There have also been reports of a few attorneys who have tried to "spirit away" pregnant women already planning an identified adoption, urging them to switch to a plan with those attorneys' clients. Any such practice would likely be strongly disapproved by the judge finalizing an eventual adoption—but only if the judge is informed of the problem.

Adoptions in Which Placement Precedes the Home Study

The greatest concerns about identified adoption primarily involve one specific type: those which are arranged independently of adoption agencies, and in which the child physically goes home with the prospective adopters *before* a home study is completed. The Child Welfare League of America opposes this practice, citing inadequate protection for the child.

A home study that takes place only after the child is placed with the prospective adopters, explains Eileen Mayers Pasztor, director of CWLA's Family Foster Care Program, can't meet the goals of child protection and family service that a preplacement home study does. One major goal—ensuring that the adopters are ready and able to nurture the child when the child arrives—has already been missed. Nor does anyone have the responsibility of following up, providing any needed services, or even ensuring that the adoption goes through as planned. Because the placement is already made, and the child might be traumatized by another move, many social workers may see their role as little more than being asked to provide a "rubber stamp" to allow the adoption. Pasztor warns that if you bring home a child without getting your home study and preparation completed first, you encourage a practice that may be dangerous to children in general—even if you feel confident that no harm is done in your own particular case. CWLA also cites concerns that if an agency is only minimally involved, needed postadoption services may be missed.

Reflecting the concerns raised, identified adoption, except through a licensed adoption agency, is illegal in Massachusetts, Connecticut, Delaware, Michigan, and North Dakota. Yet even in these states a type of identified adoption is possible. As in Ira and Kay Cohen's case, some agencies will first do a home study, and then facilitate an adoption in which the adopters find the pregnant woman, either through their own efforts or with their lawyer's assistance.

The Lawyer's Role in Identified Adoption

Almost every adoption, including a confidential one, involves a lawyer to represent you in the court process. In identified adoption, however, the lawyer's role is even more central. Important features of identified adoption, for example, include the two legal agreements: the prebirth one setting out your responsibilities and everyone's intent, and the consent to adoption and waiver of parental rights after the birth. These crucial legal documents should be prepared by a lawyer with expertise in the area. Additionally, the lawyer may fulfill some of the responsibilities traditionally performed by social workers in confidential agency adoptions, such as information gathering. In fact, the less closely you work with an agency in an identified adoption, the more closely you'll need to work with your lawyer.

A crucial aspect of the lawyer's role relates to the risk that the pregnant woman and/or the child's father may decide against adoption after you already feel emotionally and financially invested in the anticipated adoption. In every state, as already noted, the birthparents are not legally bound until they actually place the child and sign a consent to adoption. But in some states, and in some circumstances, the right to stop the adoption may continue even after a consent is signed and you take the child home. To minimize this risk, you'll need clear information about the child's legal status and full compliance with all legal requirements throughout every step of the process.

A good attorney can also help you see the situation in

perspective and not overreact to apparent setbacks. For example, while waiting for the birth of the baby they were hoping to adopt, the Cohens found themselves thrown into panic when the pregnant woman stopped returning their telephone calls. At their attorney's suggestion, they wrote her a letter saying they understood her concerns but hoped she'd get back in touch. They suggested she might want to get counseling to work through her ambivalence. She did, and the counseling ultimately helped reaffirm her commitment to agree to the adoption. They, meanwhile, had a written record showing they were not coercing her in any way.

Sometimes it is not a change of mind by the birthmother but the arrival on the scene of the birthfather that creates legal problems in a completed identified adoption. According to New York City attorney Frederick MaGovern, most identified adoption problems, at least in New York, arise out of the rights of unmarried fathers. In part this is because of a recent New York State Supreme Court ruling (which has counterparts in some other states) that no longer requires the father to have lived with the mother in order to claim his parental rights. In some cases, the adoption was completed without a consent from the birthfather but was later contested by him. MaGovern, who specializes in such contested adoptions, says adopters should be cautious if a birthmother declines to name the father. He may not know she is pregnant, or may think she plans to get an abortion.

On the plus side, remember that neither mothers nor fathers often change their minds about a planned adoption. Your attorney, by meeting and talking with both parents, can help make such a last-minute disappointment even less likely.

The lawyer, as an intermediary, can also provide a

measure of privacy by handling some of the more sensitive aspects of communicating with the pregnant woman. For example, if you'd rather not have your address known by her, payments for her medical and other expenses can be drawn on the lawyer's bank account.

Choosing a Lawyer

With so much riding on the lawyer in this process, how do you make a good choice? You can start by getting recommendations, such as from a friend or member of your adoption support group who has successfully completed an identified adoption. A local bar association group, such as the adoption subcommittee of a state family bar section, may also be helpful. Or you might read up on identified adoption at your local library, making note of lawyers in your state or region who are quoted in magazines and books on the issue. Because the field is very specialized, you'll want to choose a lawyer who has experience in the area.

Your initial meeting with the lawyer—the consultation—is often either free or reasonably priced, and you may want to interview several. During the consultation, feel free to ask whatever questions you have. These should include at least the following:

- How much experience does the lawyer have with adoption? Does he or she specialize in identified adoption? How many adoptions have been successfully completed?
- What will the lawyer charge? Typically, an attorney will charge a flat fee in an identified adoption of

anywhere from $2,000 to $6,000. Once a fee is identified, make sure you know exactly what services will be included.

- What other costs will be involved? What is the usual total cost, including all legal fees, the home study, all payments on behalf of the birthmother, all medical costs, travel, advertising, phone expenses, and any other expenses? Most identified adoptions, as noted above, are expensive, commonly costing from $10,000 to $25,000.
- Who will make the medical and any needed counseling arrangements for the pregnant woman? The attorney should be prepared to assist as needed, but without infringing on the rights of the woman involved.
- How are accounts kept and statements issued? A reputable lawyer will issue periodic account statements, allowing you to keep an eye on expenses.
- Can the lawyer handle out-of-state adoptions? Does he or she have connections, such as lawyers and doctors, in other states?
- What does the lawyer recommend in terms of communication and possible meeting with the pregnant woman before the child is born? What about after the adoption? What role will you play, and what role will the lawyer play?

The most important feature of any lawyer you choose should be strict adherence to honest and ethical practices. For example, no lawyer should encourage you to pay fees "under the table," to the lawyer or to anyone else. According to Dawn Smith-Pliner, director of Friends in Adoption, which advocates on behalf of identified adoption nationally, all fees from both the lawyer and the private adoption agency, if one is involved, must by law be accounted for in most states. Charges of illegal baby selling, she says, often arise when there is no accounting of costs, or when the fee charged exceeds reasonable costs.

Practices which are legal but ethically questionable should also be avoided. A few attorneys, as well as some unlicensed "adoption facilitators," have been known to circulate flyers among potential adopters, offering to introduce the adopters to a pregnant woman seeking adopters for a fee of up to $500. There is no guarantee the woman will choose any particular couple who responds, or any couple at all. In addition to the quick profit motive, some people believe the flyers are used by unscrupulous lawyers simply to attract identified adoption clients. In most states, though, the flyers and other such offers are completely legal forms of lawyer advertising.

Beyond mere competence and honesty, evaluate an attorney on the basis of the quality of service you feel you'll receive. Does he or she seem organized, sensitive, full of advice, and readily available? This person will be your employee, but also your partner in reaching an important and personal family goal. You should expect service, kindness, and conscientiousness, in addition to expertise. Finally, you should insist on a lawyer who shows respect for you and for the pregnant woman.

Working with an Agency

You'll also be working with an adoption agency, at least to complete a home study and possibly also to facilitate the adoption. The considerations in working with an agency will be similar to those discussed at length in Chapter 5, but you'll want to look specifically for an agency with experience in facilitating identified adoptions.

A growing number of private adoption agencies are using identified adoption techniques in their own placements. The practice of offering medical and living expenses to pregnant women, paid by the prospective adopters, is quite common. That of facilitating information exchanges, and a personal agreement between the birth- and adoptive parents, is becoming more common.

A few innovative agencies have an even more interpersonal policy. Adopters agree not only to pay the medical costs related to the birth of the child they hope to adopt, but also, sometime after the adoption, to personally house a pregnant woman until her delivery. To avoid any pressure on the pregnant women in the program, hosting is done by couples only after they have adopted the child of a different woman. This may also help keep adoption costs down, since pregnant women in the program don't have apartment, food, and transportation expenses.

To some, this arrangement is a lovely, interpersonal exchange that can help to share symbolically the birth experience. Some adopters also say that hosting a single pregnant woman helps them understand what a woman placing her child for adoption experiences. "It gave me more compassion," explained one adoptive mother. "Before, I had some negative stereotypes, but now I feel I'll be better able to talk with my daughter about her birthmother."

Some birthmothers also report that, while actively thinking about their own child's future, it can be a comfort to see the hosting couple with the child recently adopted. As one birthmother explained, "I worried about who would be raising my child, but if they're anything like Sandy and Jack [the couple who hosted her], I can see they'll be good parents."

Not everyone is so pleased. One adopting couple, Karen and Richard Timmons, say their experience with this type of arrangement was loaded with both good and bad. Despite the theoretical cost-saving feature, their adoption was still extremely expensive, costing nearly $18,000. That meant that Richard had to continue work full-time, and Karen half-time, when the baby arrived. Yet no sooner had they begun caring for the baby when the pregnant woman they had promised to host arrived. Karen says she found herself constantly on the run, taking the young woman to childbirth classes and medical visits. Happy as they are with their infant son, Karen and Richard found the arrangement an imposition and would not repeat it if adopting again.

When you call adoption agencies to discuss their services in identified adoption, be sure to ask about any programs they may have. You may want to visit a few different agencies, comparing their policies and getting a sense of how well you'd work together. At a minimum, you'll want to be sure to work with an agency with experience in identified adoption.

Making Your Search Known

In some identified adoption cases, the attorney or the adoption agency puts the prospective adopters in touch with one or more pregnant women considering adoption. Often, however, the adopters make the first contact themselves.

Three common ways to make contact with pregnant

women considering adoption are word of mouth, family autobiographies, and advertising.

Word of mouth costs nothing, but it takes guts: it involves telling anyone who'll listen of your interest in adopting and your search for a birthparent. Even if you prefer to advertise, you should still spread the word to acquaintances who have contact with pregnant women, such as clergy and doctors. Some hopeful adopters have tried it with everyone they meet—quite a conversation opener at parties.

An improvement on the word-of-mouth method is the family autobiography, a flyer that can be sent to hundreds of clinics, community centers, and houses of worship within a state or region. Each autobiography should include a cover letter that explains who you are and why you have sent the autobiography, which you hope will be posted or given to pregnant women who may be considering adoption. The autobiography should detail your interests, your marriage, why you want to adopt, and what you feel you have to offer a child. You should mention your willingness to cover reasonable expenses, and close with your phone number and an invitation to call collect.

Probably the most efficient method of reaching birthmothers is newspaper advertising. You have probably seen these ads in your local newspaper:

> *Happily married professional couple seeks to adopt healthy infant, to whom we can offer loving, secure home. Call collect anytime.*

These ads often mention the benefits that will be offered to the child and the paid medical care and expenses that the adopters will provide to the birthmother. Many begin with the word "adoption," as in:

Adoption: We want to give your newborn a loving home (and cover your medical costs). Legal and confidential. Call collect after 7 p.m. and weekends.

You can add some emotional appeal to your ad as well; for instance:

Childless couple wants to give you and your baby a happier future.

Newspaper ads are priced by the word, and you'll place a number of ads over a period of weeks. Therefore, keep the ad short. It is best not to mention some factors just yet, such as if you are single or older. That information can and should be given when a birthparent calls.

Information about race is also sensitive. Although it makes sense, for the child's benefit, to seek a racial match, specifying a child's race in an ad is tactless. You may wish, however, to state your own race in the ad, as in *Loving white couple* . . . or *Secure, caring African American couple seeks child*. . . .

Not all newspapers accept adoption ads. Smaller ones seem more likely to—and the personals section of newspapers in smaller communities is more likely to be read. There, too, birthmothers may be more reluctant to seek abortion or to keep the child. In big cities, a large number of couples may be seeking to adopt, posing the risk that your ad might get lost in a crowd.

The first step in your advertising campaign is to develop a strategy. Decide how much you want to spend and how quickly you want to spend it. Many couples expect to spend as much as $1,000 on advertising, and they often spend it rapidly, placing ads everywhere in a blitz of enthusiasm. Another method is to target only a few communities and run your ads there for a longer period. Some ads may generate more responses than others, but each should probably run for at least two weeks.

Next, choose the communities where you'll place the ads. Placing ads in out-of-state publications is fine, if your attorney is prepared to handle out-of-state adoptions and you are willing to meet the extra expenses involved. Your attorney, for example, may have to work with another lawyer in that state (in addition to any attorney representing the birthparents). You may also need to travel to the state, or even temporarily establish residence there. You can limit costs by choosing a state where you have friends you can stay with if needed. It is also wise to ask your lawyer which states are recommended.

Once you have decided on the communities where you want to place the ad, visit your local library and obtain the names and phone numbers of local newspapers. Two directories are available, the *Editor and Publisher Yearbook* and the *Gale Directory of Publications*, both of which are updated annually. Call the newspapers you have targeted and ask whether they permit adoption advertising, how much it costs, and what special rules apply. Find out also what the paper's circulation is and how many adoption ads are running currently.

When the ads run, you should receive copies of them as they appear. Check the copies for accuracy and hang onto them since some courts may want to see them later.

Responding to Callers

Whether you advertise or use word of mouth, you may wish to have a separate telephone line installed to receive calls responding to the ad. That way you can keep an answering machine on the line at all times with a special message that you might not want to use for ordinary callers. If so, order the line several weeks in advance of placing your ads, to give the phone company time to install it. Answer the phone whenever you can, but when you cannot, use a cheery taped message that begins "Hello—we are taking all collect calls" and urges the caller to please leave a phone number.

Who should answer the phone? Most couples choose the wife, assuming that a pregnant woman would want to talk to a woman. If the husband is sensitive and empathetic, though, he is just as good a choice. The pregnant woman, after all, will want to know about her child's future father at some point—and what better father is there than one who takes a role in every family responsibility? Also, many of the callers will be male.

The first call usually comes after a week or longer. When it does, you begin both a search for information and a courtship. Emphasize the latter by lending a sympathetic ear and showing complete respect for the caller.

Start by volunteering information about yourselves—a good way to encourage the caller to give you information. If you, for instance, start by revealing your own and your partner's jobs and ages, the birthparent may be encouraged to respond in kind.

Aside from age and employment, other questions you might want to ask include the following:

- When is the baby due?
- Is a doctor being consulted?
- Are there any problems in your medical history?
- Are you married?

- Do you have children?
- What is your ethnic background?
- How does the father (or mother) feel about adoption?
- How do your parents feel about adoption?
- What is your living arrangement now?
- What would you like to see happen in terms of having your child adopted?

These are just suggestions, though—don't bombard the caller with questions all at once. If you are nervous, it is fine to admit it; it may even make you seem more human and get the conversation rolling. Keep in mind that this is just the first contact, and you can save any sensitive questions for later.

Your conversation may begin to give you a sense of the risk involved, both to the child and yourselves. If the mother is under age twenty or over thirty-five, there may be health risks to the child. If she is employed, she may have medical coverage. If she has already had another child, she understands the bonds that are developed during pregnancy, and may be more likely to know if she can place her newborn for adoption.

As you talk, you'll be trying to get a sense of the woman and the child she is likely to bear. You cannot eliminate every risk, nor should you expect a guaranteed "perfect" child. It is important to ignore what birthparents look like or how educated they seem, and pay attention to relevant information such as the mother's health, health habits, and past medical history.

If cost is of concern to you, be alert to some factors that can make an identified adoption prohibitively expensive. If, for instance, the pregnant woman is out of work, has no health insurance, is not far along in the pregnancy, and lives in a state where you will first have to establish residency to adopt, the total cost will be extremely high. You might be wiser to wait than to proceed with that particular caller.

If a pregnant woman who seems unsure of her decision calls, ask if she has had a chance to discuss it with anyone, particularly the father, her parents, or a counselor. If she hasn't, encourage her to do so, since the more certain she is of her decision, the less likely she is later to revoke it. Generally, too, the father, if known, must give his consent to the adoption, so it is best to get him involved as soon as possible.

Of course, some hesitancy is to be expected. In fact, your bigger concern might be the overeager caller. Cases have been reported of callers who approach several couples, getting each to pay the same expenses. More typically, the crank caller will be a disturbed or lonely person using the phone to bring some human contact into his or her world. Try to be patient, and don't let the crank calls harden you. You'll want to stay in a receptive mood for the moment when the right call arrives.

Making a Decision

Don't feel you have to get an answer to every question you may have in the first call or even in later calls. Remember, your attorney has been through this many times before and can take on the job of gaining the more detailed information. Some use a questionnaire while interviewing a pregnant woman to ensure that no topic is missed. Your attorney should also be experienced enough to spot potential problems, such as a father who is hovering at the edge of the stage and might suddenly enter the picture.

A doctor can also play an important role in the information-gathering stage, since he or she is best able to advise to what degree any aspects of the woman's health habits or medical history place the unborn child at risk. Sometimes more tests are needed, although requests for them must be handled delicately so as not to alienate the pregnant woman.

Keep in mind that the pregnant woman is involved in a choosing process, too. Women considering adoption may call several potential adopters and ask many of the same questions. You may be asked to send pictures of yourselves, your home, even the child's room. Any decisions will and must be mutual, built on mutual respect.

Identified adoption, like all forms of adoption, involves decisions and hopes, joys and challenges. Because it is fairly new as a process and has few safeguards, it holds some specific risks. It imposes on you an extra obligation to proceed carefully, with full regard for the welfare of the child and the rights of the child's birthparents. Don't be afraid to seek help when you need it, especially from adoption support groups or social service professionals involved in adoption.

Some adopters choose to meet the pregnant woman in person, and may even be present at the birth. In some cases, the adopters and birthmother agree to exchange letters once a year, often on the child's birthday. A few birthmothers meet with their children after the adoption, sometimes throughout the child's life. Later contacts, although many prospective adopters are nervous about them, may actually be healthy and meaningful for the child. Only you can determine your own comfort level with such arrangements.

One of the most affirming aspects of identified adoption is the freedom it offers you and the birthparents, not only in choosing one another but in shaping the adoption process. You can determine what level of openness feels right for you, based on your sense of what will help you most in meeting the child's needs.

Nine

KINSHIP CARE

Kinship care, whether by a relative, a neighbor, or a friend, is one of the most important ways that we can affirm a child's family and community ties. Caring kinship providers, when available, can help enormously to preserve a child's sense of continuity and belonging.

—Eileen Mayers Pasztor
Child Welfare League of America

If the last few decades have brought incredible stress to nuclear families, they have also, in some ways, led to growth and the finding of strength in extended-family relationships. Today a greater percentage of American children live in families headed by a nonparent relative than at any other time since the Great Depression of the 1930s.

Where relatives are not available to share in a child's care, other relationships may develop to fill the gap. Neighbors, friends, and the type of child and family mentor discussed in Chapter 3 may all play an increasingly important role in a child's life. If a child needs foster care because the parents become unable to provide safe daily care, caring relatives, friends, or mentors often provide the best possible choice of caregivers.

Commonly known as kinship care, this specialized type of relationship involves the care of children by relatives or friends, after the child has entered state custody because of parental abuse, neglect, or inability to care for the child. In a sense, kinship care is as natural and obvious as community itself. It follows the age-old tradition of caring for children within a community of relatives, neighbors, and friends.

In the past generally used only as an *alternative* to foster care, kinship care has in recent years become a major and growing *type* of foster care. During the past five years, for example, the number of New York City children in kinship care surged from only 45 to more than 20,000—or over half the total foster care caseload.

Why It Is Important to Learn about Kinship Care

As common and as potentially valuable as kinship care is, many people interested in children don't think much about it as an option. In large part, this may be because we assume that no relative of ours is likely ever to need foster care. This assumption, although common, is not an entirely safe one, much as we cannot assume that our families are immune from such common problems as mental illness, alcoholism or drug problems, suicide, or domestic violence. Every family has problems, and none is entirely immune from even serious problems.

There is a second, equally important reason to learn about kinship care. Even if a child from your immediate family never needs foster care, other children you know and care about may. This is especially true if, through child and family mentoring or other volunteer activities, you are involved with children whose families are under stress. We have already seen, in the account in Chapter 3 of Gary and Hector, how a child being mentored may at some point need foster parenting, and the mentor may be best suited to provide it.

Kinship care programs and policies are just now beginning to receive the attention and priority they deserve. No longer viewed as an exceptional situation (as in Gary and Hector's case, some years ago), kinship care now constitutes a major, growing form of alternative parenting.

Often the need for foster care arises in response to a sudden emergency. A caseworker may be searching to find, before the sun sets, a safe, caring home for a child you care about. You may be asked if you'd consider becoming a kinship provider, or you may want to make the offer. A decision with enormous consequences, for your life and the life of a child, may be needed in distressingly short order.

Learning a little bit *now* about kinship care can help you *then*, if needed, to make that crucial decision. If you do become a kinship caregiver, you'll be better able, with knowledge, to obtain needed support services and to set appropriate limits. Finally, you may then have a calmer and more positive approach at a time that could otherwise feel overwhelming. This is important, because the child you care for will need your calm and reassurance.

State Kinship Care Policies

State policies about kinship care vary widely. Even the name used may vary, including, for example, "identified caretaker homes" or "relative providers." Yet most states have some mechanism (formal or informal) for identifying, and in many cases giving preference to, appropriate placements with a relative or other person who has a positive relationship with the child.

One major difference among states is the legal status accorded kinship care providers—whether they are regulated like other foster parents, and whether they receive foster care reimbursement payments. According to a U.S. Supreme Court case, *Youakim* v. *Miller*, 440 U.S. 125 (1979), states may not discriminate against extended-family members who want to be foster parents, at least if the child is eligible for federally funded foster care services. This means that if you meet your state's requirements for foster parents, you can't be arbitrarily refused as a federally reimbursed foster parent just because you are a relative or family friend.

Yet states differ in how they handle situations where the kinship provider doesn't fit into the traditional mold designed for nonrelatives. For example, suppose your niece and nephew need foster care and you'd like to provide it, but your state requires that foster parents have a separate bedroom for boys and one for girls, and your home lacks the needed space. Or suppose your state has a three- to six-month foster parent approval and licensing process, and you haven't yet enrolled—but you suddenly learn that a child you have been a mentor to for the last two years is being placed into foster care *today.* In these circumstances, what is the state's responsibility to adapt the rules, if necessary, to make a kinship care placement available to the child? A few states, such as New York, Illinois, and Michigan, have laws and regulations designed to encourage kinship care as an official form of foster care. In these states, kinship providers are encouraged and given reimbursement payments like any other foster parents. There is, however, a highly streamlined emergency approval process, with certain less important rules relaxed or waived as needed.

Other states may place children with relatives or family friends who don't meet all the requirements to be foster parents, but not classify or reimburse them as foster parents. In the best such programs, the social services department will at least provide any useful or needed services to the kinship caregiver, such as day care or after-school care, a rent supplement (if needed to move to an apartment with enough room for the children), and so on.

Many states, unfortunately, have no consistent policy regarding kinship providers and rely solely on case-by-case decision making. Or they may have one set of policies for relatives, and a different policy, or no policy, for nonrelated persons already involved in the child's life.

If at some point you are considering becoming a kinship caregiver, find out about your state's policies from the office placing the child or children involved. If you have any questions about whether they are fair and reasonable, whether they adequately protect the child and the parents, and whether they provide the service or financial supports you may need to adequately care for the child, discuss the issue with a local attorney specializing in child welfare law. Some legal services offices, providing free legal services to lower-income families, have been particularly active in working to improve agency handling of these cases.

Opportunities and Challenges

The most important potential advantage of kinship care is the sense of continuity and belonging it can provide to children. It can help address one of the major difficulties that foster care often imposes on children: the feeling that they are being thrust into strange situations with people they don't know and who may or may not stay in their lives. Kinship care, by contrast, allows the child to remain, if not in the parental home, at least with a known and familiar person. Additionally (and you can help to emphasize this), the child has the affirmation of knowing that the kinship care provider made a specific commitment, based on affection for *that particular child.* The child can say, in effect, "I was wanted for *me.*"

If you become a kinship caregiver, the arrangement may offer the special pleasure of sharing family-style closeness with a child or children who are already a part of your life. It may also be easier to judge your ability to care for children whom you already know and like, and whose needs and behaviors you understand.

At the same time, there are special challenges to kinship care. Families are wonderful, the best known way to raise children. But anyone who's ever been in one knows that families can be confusing, painful, and messy. Even healthy families are complicated, and families under stress may be more complex still. It is a fact of life.

Kinship care can place one at the heart of extended-family life. This is especially true if the kinship provider is a relative, but it can also be true with a caring friend or mentor. Kinship care can involve a web not only of caring and shared joy but also of mutual hurts and anxieties.

In some ways, kinship care has the potential to be the best, most nurturing form of foster care for the child—and the most challenging for the kinship provider. You'll be challenged not only to meet the child's daily needs but to do so in a context that affirms all the child's relationships. The result can be deeply affirming for you as well.

Loyalty and Anger

In their well-kept home in a mid-size Ohio city, Bella and Jim Walters seem far from big-city problems. The parents of four grown children, they feel fortunate that most of the family still lives nearby. For twenty-two years, they have run not only a family but a family restaurant together.

As in most families, the passing years have brought a mix of joys and troubles: four high school graduations, three college admissions, one drug arrest, one premarital and one nonmarital pregnancy, two college graduations, five grandchildren, three marriages, and one divorce. Yet nothing quite prepared them for the day a social worker called them about their grandchildren Dana and Lizzie.

"I *knew* there were problems," says Jim, "and I tried to talk with my daughter Mary about it. I could tell she was a drinker, and who knows what all, and then her husband up and left her pregnant with their second child. I told her you've got responsibilities, you can't be out carousing like a teenager. But did she listen? Of course not."

Drinking, as it turned out, was only part of the problem. When the baby, Lizzie, was born, she was underweight and premature, and remained for a week in the neonatal care unit. Mary, who was released from the hospital, was reported by hospital staff to be jittery and unusually distracted in her manner. Suspecting drug involvement, hospital staff tested the baby's urine and found it positive for prenatal cocaine exposure. The state social services department was contacted, and a worker made an unscheduled visit to Mary's home. Finding four-year-old Dana alone in the apartment, the worker took emergency custody of both children, which was affirmed by a court the next day.

"It was Mary [who showed up shortly after the worker had arrived] who told the social worker to call us," explains Bella. "And we were grateful for that at least. So we said thank you, of course we'll take the children, and we can take it from here. After all, it wasn't the first time our grandchildren had stayed with us, and, frankly, we felt it was a private family matter."

To Bella and Jim's initial dismay, it wasn't quite that simple. As the social worker explained, this was a child protection matter, and the state had temporary legal custody now. The agency had a responsibility both to see that the children were safe in their temporary home and to help make a permanent plan.

"Well, we were furious," says Bella. "Looking back, maybe we were as much furious with the whole situation, with our daughter, with the drugs, with what had happened to Dana and Lizzie. But, at the time, I'd say our anger was mostly focused on the social worker, and what we saw as the very nerve of the whole idea. I mean, here was this social worker, we said, all of maybe twenty-five or thirty, and she's telling us how to raise our grandchildren!"

Today, a year later, Bella and Jim have achieved an uneasy peace with the social worker and the system. "She has helped," admits Jim grudgingly, "because I'm not sure we could have been as firm with Mary as she was. Basically, Mary was told 'Get drug treatment and get straight, or the kids aren't coming back.' I don't know if we could have done that. We always want to see the best; we might have believed Mary's promises when we shouldn't. But I can't pretend it's been comfortable having a stranger involved in our life like this."

Mary, too, has mixed feelings about the arrangement. After a one-month in-patient drug treatment program, Mary has continued to receive therapy and to participate in Nar-Anon, a self-help group for drug abusers based on the principles of Alcoholics Anonymous. She feels both grateful and resentful that her children are being cared for by her parents, and both eager and nervous to have them return to her care.

To help make the transition, the children began spending overnights with their mother shortly after the in-patient treatment was completed, and have gradually progressed to spending three nights a week. Tentatively, the children are scheduled to come home—but with frequent visits to their grandparents—next month.

Occasionally, at Mary's request, her mother joins her in her weekly therapy session. There they try to address their concerns, both as mother and daughter to each other, and as grandmother and mother of Dana and Liz.

"We've loved having Dana and Lizzie with us," says Jim. "And, honestly, I have to say it's been the best possible solution. This whole situation hasn't been easy for the children. Even being with us, Dana misses her mother, and Lizzie seems to have some medical and behavioral problems because of the prenatal cocaine exposure. But I think it's been good for them, and for all of us, to be in this together as a family."

The Role of the Social Services Department

The role of the social services department in a kinship care arrangement is a delicate one. Its primary role is to ensure that the child is protected and the child's family served. Additionally, as Bella and Jim's experience shows, the department can supply a measure of control and leverage in promoting positive family change.

Unfortunately, the line between necessary supervision and unnecessary intrusion may be a fine one. You may find, if you become a kinship care provider, that it is often difficult, both for the caseworker and for you, to determine when the line has been crossed. You may, for example, feel uncomfortable with the fact that a social worker is involved at all. If you are asked to participate in any form of therapy with the child's parents, you may feel criticized and judged.

Although these concerns are natural and reasonable, it is a good idea to try to moderate them somewhat. Asking for more information, such as a clear explanation of the goals of any proposed training, therapy, or services, is an excellent beginning.

If you believe that a proposed course of action is unwise, or feel that a caseworker is failing to work with you in a professional manner, by all means raise your concerns.

Similarly, you should feel free to push for services that you think are needed but are not being provided. Either way, try always to keep your focus on what will benefit the child—even if it means giving up a little bit of your own privacy.

Suppose, for example, that a caseworker says to you that you and the child's mother seem to be constantly competing for the child's affections, and you feel criticized by the remark. It is perfectly fair to ask, "Are there things you think I'm doing well? It's easier for me to hear concerns in a positive context." At the same time, whether or not you think the caseworker's observation was well presented, consider whether there is a particle of truth to it. If so, it is worth putting some energy into resolving the issue. Remember, the caseworker will be gone from your life in time, but the child's needs will continue. If attending some therapy sessions or accepting some services may benefit the child, that is a good reason to do so.

This does not mean, however, that you have the responsibility to help "fix" the children's parents. You can be encouraging, you can provide a good example, and you can and will help by caring for the children during the time of need. But in kinship care, as in any other form of foster parenting, you are not responsible for making the parent healthy—no matter if the parent is your adult child, your sibling, or your friend. The parent, with the help of services provided, has that responsibility.

For this reason, the caseworker assigned to help the family can and should help relieve you of this responsibility, even if you have tried to take it on in the past. As the experience of a Boston area couple shows, this can be a substantial relief. It can also help focus, clarify, and improve your relationship with the child.

An Activist for Children

Ask Pam Kelsey what kind of work she does, and her answer is quick and cheerful: "I'm a parent and a neighborhood activist." In addition to these constants in her life, she has, over the past several years, worked part-time as a local newspaper reporter, a bookkeeper at a local nursing home, and, most recently, as a licensed day-care provider. Mike Brown, her husband, is a science editor for the Massachusetts Institute of Technology, while also placing a high priority on family life. Their home, in a middle-income family neighborhood of Boston, has a warm, friendly atmosphere.

The event that brought Anji Chowderi, then age ten, into their life was age-old kid stuff: Anji, who lived in the neighborhood, was being roughhoused by the neighborhood bully. Pam saw it, got mad, and took action. She ran outside, gave the older child a stern scolding, and set about comforting Anji and bandaging her scrapes. Then, because Anji was still shaky, she walked her home, where she met Anji's mother.

Over time the friendship with Anji grew. Anji drifted over to Mike and Pam's house often, and Pam would call Anji's mother to ask if the child might stay to visit. The answer, listlessly offered, was always yes.

Anji's mother, it soon became clear, was deeply depressed, probably to the point of needing medical and psychological help. An immigrant from the more traditional culture of Pakistan, she had never adjusted to American culture and spoke little English. She had few or no local friends, and had been devastated when Anji's father left them. She was not employed, nor even particularly active in raising Anji. As for Anji's father, he was remarried and living in another state, did not want custody, and chose not to be in contact with Anji or her mother.

A responsible child, Anji chose her own clothes, ate mostly sandwiches or canned food, and kept the house neat. What she couldn't provide for herself, of course, was what every child needs and deserves: a home filled with caring and nurturance. So, following a healthy instinct, she had found and chosen in Pam and Mike a family happier and healthier than her own. Bilingual and extremely bright, Anji also enjoyed the intellectual stimulation that Pam and Mike offered.

For Pam, in particular, the fondness was mutual. Much of Pam's day was spent with the couple's two preschoolers; by comparison, Anji seemed like semiadult company. And because the two preschoolers were boys, Anji's presence made Pam feel less like a lone female in an otherwise male household. Most important, Anji was simply a lovely person. Before long, Pam and Anji developed a warm friendship that was as much sisterly as parental. And as Anji approached her teen years, Pam and Mike began hiring her as a babysitter.

Bit by bit, over a period of about three years, Anji was becoming a part of the family. With her mother's ever more listless blessing, she was staying for more and more lunches, then dinners, then overnights. For Mike and Pam, it was both a pleasure and a worry. They liked her, even loved her, but wondered if they were doing the right thing.

Repeatedly, Pam tried to befriend Anji's mother, to get her involved in the world (or at least Anji's world), and to help her obtain medical help and/or counseling to address what was clearly disabling depression. Although courteous, Mrs. Chowderi rebuffed Pam's efforts, denying any problem.

Worse, Mrs. Chowderi was increasingly refusing to care for Anji. Finally, just after Anji turned thirteen, her mother told her she didn't want her living at home anymore.

By that time, Pam was pregnant with what they had planned would be their third and last child, and Anji had more or less moved into the room they had planned for the baby. Although they had third-floor space they could convert to a room for Anji, it was hard to know whether that made sense in such an undefined relationship. Money, too, was tight: counting Anji, they were looking toward supporting six people on one-and-a-half salaries. Anji's mother was apparently receiving either AFDC or child support for Anji, but they were largely raising her.

Finally, they were concerned and uncomfortable about their legal status. Suppose Anji needed emergency medical care, and they couldn't reach her mother? What if Mrs. Chowderi allowed Anji's health care coverage to lapse? Suppose Mrs. Chowderi's emotional condition changed, and she accused them of kidnapping the child or alienating her affections? Much as they loved Anji, they felt a growing responsibility had emerged, with no clear definition or direction.

Anji, too, showed signs of anxiety and ambivalence. Thriving on the warmth and stimulation that Pam and Mike and their two young sons offered, she began dropping hints that she wished she could live there always. Yet knowing that there was no guarantee, she felt wary; at times, she acted cold and aloof to Mike, in particular, or seemed jealous of the boys. With Mike and Pam's encouragement, she successfully tested into the prestigious Boston Latin public high school—

but was caught clumsily stealing from Pam's wallet that same week. She seemed to be testing their tolerance, finding out if they'd send her away.

At that point, Pam and Mike realized the toll that unclear expectations was taking on all of them. Gathering information, first from a lawyer specializing in children's welfare issues, then from a privately employed social worker, they began to weigh their options. Learning that Massachusetts, like many states, favors choosing relatives or known friends as foster care providers, they weighed the possibility of seeking help from the state social services department in making a permanent plan for Anji.

They agreed that they would be most comfortable either acting as Anji's kinship caregivers, or, if it were possible, helping Anji's mother to address her problems so Anji could return there. They ruled out adoption because it could provoke or alienate Anji's parents, further cutting her off from them, as well as compromise her ability to qualify for college scholarships based on financial need.

The next decision was whom to talk with first: Anji, her mother, or a representative of the department. With some hesitation, they decided to go to the department first. It seemed unfair to raise Anji's expectations—and unwise to approach Anji's mother—until their options were clear.

Their contact was handled by the department as a complaint of child abandonment. Initially, the social worker who met with them at their home was unhelpful. "Since Anji is basically living with you," he said, "and by all reports is doing well, she's not abandoned or neglected. There's really nothing we can do."

Pam, characteristically, decided on a direct, even blunt approach. "Let me be clear," she said. "She can't stay unless we establish our legal role. If you find, as I think you will, that her mother can't or won't care for her, we'll be happy to act as her foster parents. But it's not fair for us or for her to have her stay in limbo, with her mother having custody but no real role."

In effect, as hard as it was for Pam to say it, she and Mike were offering the department a choice: open a case for Anji while she remained with them, or open the case under worse circumstances, because they would not keep her under a cloud of uncertainty.

"I'm sorry," explains Pam, remembering the conversation, "but that child *had* been abandoned. The department has a responsibility, and it doesn't help anyone to collude with their ignoring it."

Their view prevailed, and ultimately led to a more secure situation for everyone involved. Since Anji's mother seemed to trust Pam, Pam agreed to meet together with her and the social worker assigned to the family. Mrs. Chowderi repeated that she didn't feel she could care for Anji and wanted her to stay with Mike and Pam.

By voluntary agreement, the department took custody of Anji and placed her into kinship care with Mike and Pam. (The state's actual term for the arrangement was "foster care by identified caretaker.") Because Mike and Pam did not plan to provide foster care to other children, and were already doing so well caring for Anji, they were not required to attend foster parent training.

Thanks to the changed legal status, Anji is now covered by Medicaid, and Pam and Mike receive foster care payments to help them meet the cost of her care. Mrs. Chowderi has been offered mental health services, parenting classes, and job training; although she hasn't participated in any services yet, Pam at least feels relieved that the options are there, and are no longer her responsibility to find and offer. If it turns out that Mrs. Chowderi is disabled and unemployable because of her mental state, the caseworker has explained, she'll be eligible to receive Medicaid and social security disability benefits.

Most important, the entire family, and Anji especially, knows that the arrangement is official and reflects a long-term commitment. So long as Anji is a minor, and Mrs. Chowderi remains unable or unwilling to care for her, her place in Pam and Mike's family will continue.

A reflection of Anji's increased sense of belonging became clear when Pam gave birth to Shawn, their third son. Far from being jealous, Anji seemed dreamily pleased.

"You know," she said, curled up beside Pam and the baby, "Shawn doesn't know our family any way but with me. To him, it will just be natural that I'm here."

Meeting the Child's Need to Feel Welcome and Secure

Many people assume that when a family extends to include a child who is a relative or friend, the new child will automatically feel welcome and at home. Yet this isn't always the case. In fact, although children do tend to feel more at home in familiar settings and with familiar people, they still need help understanding the changes that are taking place.

Children entering kinship care, like children entering other forms of foster care, need explanations of what is happening and why. They may also need support in grieving the loss of the birthparent's daily presence, as well as in working through any trauma over the events that led to the need for placement. This can be difficult for kinship caregivers who also may be feeling grief over the family problems. That's one reason why child and family therapy can be particularly useful in some cases.

Don't assume that if the adults view the extended-family group as "one big happy family," so will the children. A child entering kinship care may, in fact, harbor significant concerns and anxieties. These may not be directly voiced by the child, but nonetheless are important to explore.

For example, a child who goes to live with cousins or other children whom he knows and likes may nonetheless have mixed feelings. Because the other children remain with their own parents, are siblings to each other, and have not been uprooted, the new child may feel isolated or different—and humiliated by the difference. He or she may fear being a "charity case," or be ashamed of the parent's problems. The other children, who know more of the family history than new foster siblings might, may even use sensitive information as a taunt at times.

The child may also have serious concerns about the future, and may not view the current situation as being stable. This may be especially true if the long-range plans for care of the child actually are uncertain; for example, if the child's mother is involved in drug treatment or psychiatric hospitalization, and may or may not regain the ability to care for the child. Yet it may even be true in cases where the adults involved view the child's current living situation as likely to be permanent.

In dealing with children's unstated and often hidden concerns, silence is not golden. One young man, raised by his aunt and uncle almost continuously throughout his youth, recalls today the years he spent deeply hurt that his aunt and uncle never adopted him. As a result, his childhood years were filled with anxiety that he would be returned to the care of his mother, who he knew from experience was too mentally ill to care for him well. Finally, as an adult, he asked his aunt why they hadn't adopted him.

"Why, we knew you'd always be with us," she said, both surprise and fondness in her voice. "Everyone knew your mother would never be well enough to take you back, although no one wanted to say it. I did ask your mother once if she'd agree to an adoption, but she flew into a rage. I could have pushed it, but what was the point? It would only cause a legal battle and a huge family fight, and there was no reason to get into all that. As far as we were concerned, we were family and you were one of us. Everyone knew that."

"Everyone" knew, but *no one told him.* He never said a word—children often don't, for fear the very question will cause the feared losses to happen—but suffered years of needless anxiety. Only as an adult did he finally get the reassurance that would have helped him through those difficult years.

Resources That Can Help

Some of the emotional challenges posed by kinship care, such as the need to clearly inform children what is happening and how they'll be cared for, may require nothing more than careful and conscientious effort. Other issues, such as general stress or controlling children's behavioral difficulties, may be effectively addressed through general foster parenting resources such as foster parent training and support groups. In some child welfare programs, training or support groups specifically for kinship care providers are now being organized or developed. Such specialized supports may be especially helpful in addressing common concerns.

Where interfamily problems are deep-rooted, flexible forms of family counseling may be useful. Therapy can help, for example, to coordinate the efforts of the parents and the kinship providers, and to provide an extended-family context for addressing individual problems. It can also help address any conflicts that may arise centered around the care of the children. Sometimes, when a parent or other family member has refused to get help in the past, the kinship care arrangement may provide a new context and new impetus for addressing existing crucial problems.

Be aware that it is absolutely natural, at times, to feel anger, frustration, and sadness—about the situation, the children's parents, even the children. These may be signs that you need help and support in addressing your feelings and concerns, but you needn't see them as signs of failure. In kinship care, you provide to the child the complex richness of family life—which, by definition, includes its challenges.

The Promise of Kinship Care

Anji Chowderi's comment that "it will just be natural that I'm here" is at the heart of what is best about kinship care. It *is* natural that, when parents become unable to care for a child, other adults who know and care about the child step in.

The need for daily care may last from a few weeks to the rest of the child's youth. It may be provided informally, given the legal status of foster care, or even lead to permanent guardianship or adoption.

Yet, if circumstances vary, one common link remains. For a child, kinship care provides an opportunity to always be with those whom the child sees as family—even when separated from parents.

Appendix

The following groups offer information, support, and advocacy relating to foster parenting, adoption, and/or child welfare:

Emotional Support, Information, and Advocacy

National Foster Parent Association
226 Kilts Drive
Houston, TX 77024
(713) 467-1850

National support organization for foster parents and their families. Referral to state and local chapters. Newsletter, information services.

Adoptive Families of America (formerly OURS)
3333 Highway 100 North
Minneapolis, MN 55422
(612) 535-4829

National support organization for adoptive families and prospective adoptive families. Advocates for adoption legislation on state and national levels. Has local support groups around U.S.

Latin American Parents Association
P.O. Box 339
Brooklyn, NY 11234
(718) 236-8689

Support group with chapters throughout the country for those planning or having completed adoption of children from Latin America. Resources for providing a connection to child's culture of birth.

Resolve Inc.
1310 Broadway
Somerville, MA 02144
(617) 623–0744

Nonprofit organization offering support, advocacy, and education on fertility issues. Offers quarterly newsletter, extensive literature list, and referrals to other members with similar problems.

Concerned United Birthparents (CUB)
2000 Walker Street
Des Moines, IA 50317
(515) 263–9558
(800) 822–2777

A national support and advocacy group for birthmothers and birthfathers who have placed a child for adoption. Publishes newsletter.

Service, Education, and Advocacy in Foster Care and Adoption

Foster Grandparent Program
ACTION
1100 Vermont Avenue, NW
Washington, DC 20525
(202) 634–9349

Volunteer organization offering opportunities for limited income persons over age 60 to become involved in child and family mentoring.

National Resource Center on Family-Based Services
University of Iowa
112 North Hall
Iowa City, IA 52242
(319) 335–2000

Primarily a resource for programs assisting families. Offers training, technical assistance, and program evaluation. Extensive resource library and directory benefits individuals seeking programs as well.

National Resource Center for Family Support Programs
200 South Michigan, Suite 1520
Chicago, IL 60604
(312) 341-0900

Research, education, and publications on services designed to strengthen and affirm families. Good resource for locating, developing, or improving child and family mentoring programs.

National Foster Care Resource Center
Eastern Michigan University
Ypsilanti, MI 48197
(313) 487–0374

Resources for improving training and services in foster care programs. National center for research in the field. Extensive publications list.

National Adoption Center (NAC)
1218 Chestnut Street
Philadelphia, PA 19107
(215) 925–0200

Works for improved adoption opportunities, especially for special needs children. Operates national electronic referral network. Promotes adoption awareness through conferences and training programs for adoption professionals.

National Committee For Adoption
1930 17th Street NW
Washington, DC 20009
(202) 328–1200

Offers advocacy and information on adoption. Has member agencies across U.S., including private adoption agencies.

American Adoption Congress
1000 Connecticut Avenue NW, Suite 9
Washington, DC 20036
(202) 483–3399

Advocates for legislation to make adoption records open to adoptees and for adoption reform. Offers assistance in birthfamily searches.

North American Council on Adoptable Children (NACAC)
1825 University Avenue West, Suite N-498
St. Paul, MN 55104
(612) 644–3036

Works with parent support groups around the U.S. and Canada to advocate for special needs adoption. Offers training seminars on issues related to special needs adoption, such as postadoption subsidies. Brochures and annual conferences of social workers and parents.

Comprehensive Child Welfare Political Advocacy

Children's Defense Fund
25 E Street NW
Washington, DC 20001
(202) 628–8787

Public membership organization that provides strong political advocacy on a range of prochild issues and initiatives, including adoption, foster parenting, and other family welfare issues. Extensive publications list, monthly newsletter, yearly conference.

Association of Child Advocates
10 E. Main Street, Suite 101
Victor, NY 14564
(716) 924–0300

National grassroots organization dedicated to local, state, and national political advancement of children's rights.

Child Welfare League of America (CWLA)
440 First Street NW, Suite 310
Washington, DC 20001
(202) 638–2952

Advocates for adoption and foster care standards, improved services, and child welfare legislation. Excellent resource for published information. Member agencies include state adoption and foster care programs. Newsletter, yearly conference.

American Public Welfare Association
810 First Street NW, Suite 500
Washington, DC 20001
(202) 682–0100

Advocates for improved child welfare programs, through education, research, and legislation. Works with and on behalf of state departments of social services.

Legal Resources

NOTE: None of these organizations can provide legal advice in an individual case, but they may be helpful as general resources.

National Association of Counsel for Children
1205 Oneida
Denver, CO 80220
(303) 321–3963

Professional organization of attorneys and others working in the child welfare field, with nationwide membership. May be useful for identifying lawyers with expertise in adoption and child welfare.

National Center for Youth Law
114 Sansome Street, Suite 900
San Francisco, CA 94104
(415) 543–3307

Research and writing on child welfare legal issues, in addition to representation in important California cases. Publishes a newsletter.

ABA Center on Children and the Law
1800 M Street NW, Suite 220 South
Washington, DC 20036
(202) 331–2250

Resource center engaged in legal research, writing, and training to improve the justice system as it relates to children. May be able to provide assistance to attorneys in child welfare cases.

Index

INDEX